CONTEMPORARY SOCIOLOGY
OF THE SCHOOL

SARA DELAMONT
Interaction in the classroom
Second edition

MICHAEL STUBBS
Language, schools and classrooms
Second edition

ed. SARA DELAMONT
Readings on interaction in the classroom

eds MICHAEL STUBBS and HILARY HILLIER
Readings on language, schools and classrooms

SARA DELAMONT

Interaction
in
the
classroom

Second edition

First published in 1976 by Methuen & Co. Ltd
Second edition 1983
Reprinted 1985

Reprinted 1990, 1992 by Routledge
11 New Fetter Lane, London EC4P 4EE

Simultaneously published in the USA and Canada
by Routledge
a division of Routledge, Chapman and Hall, Inc.
29 West 35th Street, New York, NY 10001

© 1976 and 1983 Sara Delamont

Photoset by Rowland Phototypesetting Ltd,
Bury St Edmunds, Suffolk

Printed in Great Britain by
Richard Clay Ltd,
Bungay, Suffolk

British Library Cataloguing in Publication Data

Delamont, Sara
    Interaction in the classroom.—2nd ed.—
    (Contemporary sociology of the school)
    1. Teacher–student relationships
    2. Teachers—Great Britain
    3. Students—Great Britain
    I. Title   II. Series
    371.1′02   LB1033

    ISBN 0–415–05122–3

Library of Congress Cataloging in Publication Data

Delamont, Sara, 1947–
    Interaction in the classroom.
    (Contemporary sociology of the school)
    Bibliography: p.
    Includes index.
    1. Interaction analysis in education.
    2. Classroom management.
    I. Title   II. Series
    LB1084.D44   1983   371.1′02   83–7948

    ISBN 0–415–05122–3

Contents

Editor's introduction

When the 'Contemporary Sociology of the School' series was conceived, its purpose was to bring together the new and often complex sociological explorations of events in and around the school and its classrooms in a way in which they could be understood and made use of by teachers and other professional workers. An important part of the purpose was also to bring together, with similar clarity, the relevant range of theoretical orientations and research strategies, for without these any new understanding could only be incomplete. The enterprise has been an outstanding success. With the help of an able and enthusiastic team of authors, a group of books has been produced which has been used by tens of thousands of students. The distinctive red volumes have become key texts in their own right in universities and colleges throughout the world.

There is little doubt that the series has made an important contribution to sweeping away many of the misleadingly easy and often unexamined assumptions of the 1960s – such as those about the achievements of working-class children, girls and members of ethnic minorities. The books have illustrated the ways in which individual teacher's and student's definitions of situations can influence events, how perceptions of achievement can not only define achievement itself but also identify those who achieve; how expectations about schooling can help to determine the nature and evaluations of schools.

The books explore the main areas of the sociology of the school in which new understandings of events are available. Each introduces the reader to the new interpretations, juxtaposes them against the longer standing perspectives and reappraises the contemporary practices of education and its consequences. Each author in the series has worked extensively in his or her areas of specialism and has been encouraged not only to introduce the reader to the subject but also to develop, where appropriate, his or her own analyses of the issues. Yet though each volume has its distinctive critical approach, the themes and treatments of all of them are closely interrelated. The series as a whole is offered to students who seek understanding of the practice of education in present-day societies, and to those who wish to know how contemporary sociological theory may be applied to the educational issues of those societies.

A new development in the series is the introduction of 'readers' to accompany several of the volumes. These contain a range of papers, many not previously published, which have been selected by the authors of the original volumes to augment and develop their analyses and to help readers to extend their understanding of the fields.

Since the publication of the earlier volumes the pace of research and theoretical development in many of the areas has been rapid – development in which the authors themselves have been actively involved. This development has been particularly rapid in the study of classroom interaction. In this volume Sara Delamont has revised and rewritten her text which was first published in 1976. She has taken account of much new work of sociologists, anthropologists and ethnographers. In particular she has been able to include a range of new material based upon her own research in classrooms – in her participation in the ORACLE project at Leicester University and elsewhere. This has enabled her to develop still further the series of first-hand accounts of classrooms that were such a distinctive and popular feature of the first edition. She uses these accounts to illustrate clearly the vital but often hidden negotiations about control, knowledge and the social system that take place in every classroom. The book offers rich new insights to all who teach in classrooms and to all who study social interaction.

John Eggleston

Preface and acknowledgements

The first edition of this book not only produced complimentary reviews, it also generated a large number of letters from both strangers and friends. I hope that all those people who enjoyed and used the 1976 edition will find that this new version still meets with their approval and serves their needs. A large amount of research has been published in the sociological/ anthropological/ethnographic tradition since the first edition was written in 1974/5, so I was delighted to be able to prepare a new edition. I have tried to include a fair picture of contemporary research but not fall into the trap of overburdening the text with references. The reader unfamiliar with the area will find an annotated 'Further reading' section with details of some studies not cited in the text. The collection of readings which now accompanies this book has also allowed me to cover some of the fascinating material to have come out since 1976 (Delamont, 1984).

In 1976 I announced firmly that:

> Throughout this book I refer to teachers, researchers, and other professionals as 'she' unless the context is masculine. As the teaching profession is overwhelmingly female and I am a female researcher it seems a perverse form of false consciousness to use 'he' except where absolutely necessary.

Since that time more research has been published on the educational experiences of women, and a certain amount of 'consciousness-raising' has taken place in sociology and education. The use of 'she' whenever possible has been retained to continue that process.

Since 1976 I have been lucky enough to participate in the SSRC-funded ORACLE project at Leicester University, which enabled me to spend time observing life in four English schools, very different from those previously studied in Scotland. I am grateful to the staff and pupils of all the schools where I have been allowed to do research since 1968; especially those at 'St Luke's', 'Guy Mannering', 'Gryll Grange', 'Waverly' and 'Melin Court'. All teachers, pupils and schools have been protected by pseudonyms throughout the book. During the ORACLE research, I was aided by the enthusiasm of Brian Simon and Maurice Galton for the data I gathered.

I wish to thank Paul Atkinson for continuing to be both my toughest critic and my most encouraging colleague. Gerry Bernbaum and Tom Whiteside remain my intellectual mentors in the sociology of education. The last seven years have seen the growth of a supportive network of school and classroom ethnographers, and all its members will find their ideas in what follows. In particular, Louis M. Smith, Martyn Hammersley, Brian Davies and David Hargreaves made useful suggestions for improvements. The defects and *lacunae* in the volume remain, of course, my own.

Mrs Audrey Dunning typed the original edition of the book, and Mrs Myrtle Robins prepared this new edition for the printers. Both deserve thanks for their professional skill and dedication.

Finally I want to dedicate this book to the memory of Jocelyn Cadbury, who died in July 1982 while this edition was being prepared. Though not himself a professional social scientist he, like other members of his family, was a supporter of scholarship in the social sciences. He was always pleased to hear of research and publication by his friends, and would have been glad to know a second edition of this book had appeared.

1 Introduction

Imagine a large, stately Edwardian building set in pleasant grounds on a hilltop in an expensive residential suburb. Go through the green double doors into a panelled hall, and up the spiral staircase to the first floor. Follow the panelled corridor to the north-east corner of the building, and enter the room situated there. It is cold. The central heating must either be faulty, or someone has turned it down very low. There are four large windows facing north and east, so the room is light but not sunny. The walls are pale yellow, with a photographic reproduction of the Parthenon frieze round near the ceiling. One wall is lined with locked cupboards, and the glass fronted bookcases are also locked. Two noticeboards display information about forthcoming events to raise charitable funds and instructions in case of fire, power cuts or illness. It is very quiet. No one in the room moves or speaks, though occasional shouts can be heard from outside. Three teenage girls are sitting bent over their books, while an elderly spinster sits facing them, intent on her work.

Now imagine a completely different building – modern, sprawling, all glass and concrete. Surrounded by a sea of mud, it seems to play hide and seek among the council houses as you approach up a winding drive. Go in through a plate glass door, avoiding a coffee queue, pass a display of pottery, and turn down a corridor lined with brightly coloured lockers. The corridor stretches for about fifty yards, but keep going to the end, and go out through the door at the far end, reinforced with wire. Cross an asphalt square and enter a mobile building. This room too is cold, but also dark, for the small windows are deep in the shadows thrown by the parent building. The floor is dirty – dust and papers from crisps, sweets, and chips, blow about when you open the door. A man in his twenties is shouting and gesticulating at the front of the room. Three West Indian girls are gossiping loudly in one corner. As you enter they shout 'Who are you?', 'What do you want?' Four small, scruffy teenage boys play cards in the far left-hand corner. Another dozen teenagers, mostly small and poorly clad, watch the young man with passive non-involvement.

By now, unless you are the proverbial visitor from Mars, you will have recognized both these rooms from the pen portraits just painted. If you were to walk into them you would 'know' at once that both are classrooms. In each case I asked you to imagine walking through a school and into a classroom, and in both cases you will have spotted the intention very quickly and recognized the two situations as essentially 'the same'. Yet this is, on the surface at least, very odd. The two buildings are clearly different and the activity taking place in the classrooms equally distinct, but no one with any experience of schooling can fail to perceive their essential similarity.

This book is going to present a theoretical framework for understanding classroom interaction which is general enough to encompass both the classes characterized above, and any other classroom which the average member of western society would recognize as such. The framework is designed to be as far-reaching as our intuitive sense of what constitutes a classroom. In addition, it will be argued that previous approaches to the study of classrooms have not been all-encompassing enough and so are flawed. The framework will be presented in an abstract way, but will be illustrated with material from all types of classrooms with the appropriate research strategies for implementation spelled out.

This may sound like a tall order, for the two situations sketched above are so different. Both are drawn from field notes taken while I was observing classroom processes, but most of the variables normally controlled in educational research are as different as they could be. The first scenario is drawn from St Luke's, a girls' public school in Scotland, where I carried out participant observation over half a term. The data collected during that fieldwork are used throughout this book. The second scene was recorded in a mixed comprehensive, Sanditon College, in the English midlands, which I visited several times to observe classes. (All schools, teachers, and pupils have been given pseudonyms in this book.)

Classroom privacy was common. Most adults in Britain had their education in private classrooms, but many children in school now are experiencing learning in public situations. Architecturally 'open' education is increasingly common. Alongside my two scenarios I ought, therefore, to place a third as follows.

Imagine driving through a copse to a wooden and glass building set on a hill overlooking a mining village. Go in through glass doors, past a display of woodcarving and metalwork, and head for the south-east corner of the building. A large notice says 'Laboratories', and you can smell science. The noise is striking, too – voices and moving feet and apparatus being handled. Four rooms stand around a central hall, but all the doors are fastened open and people are milling backwards and forwards around and between them. There are lots of windows, the outer doors are open, and it is sunny and warm. About eighty adolescents are busy in the area. They refer to duplicated sheets to guide them in making shoe polish and cosmetics, cutting up rats and analysing proprietary foods. Five adults in white coats move around talking to groups and individuals and doing routine tasks. When you arrive no one notices because you are just another person in a bustling environment.

Again, this is recognizably a school, with teaching going on, based round several laboratories. We can pin the labels 'teachers' and 'pupils' on to the appropriate people, although one of the adults is really a 'technician' and closer inspection shows more routine work and less interaction with pupils. But, despite the physical differences (which are important and will be considered in detail below), this too is obviously a classroom. I argue later that the same basic framework of analysis applies. There are differences. If the classics teacher sat in silence for a whole lesson, or the maths student hit one of the card players, it is possible that no other teacher would ever know. If the chemistry student attached to the science team in the third school withdraws from interaction by silence, or lashes out at a pupil, it is visible to professional colleagues. There may well be complex repercussions. Against this, there are many points of resemblance between the third school – Mansbridge – and the other two. Work is being done in classics and science, but not in maths. Sanditon and Mansbridge are mixed comprehensives in the English midlands serving comparable catchment areas, and so on. The similarities and dissimilarities are kaleidoscopic.

Obviously a framework which will encompass all these complexities is going to be general. However, as long as we recognize something essentially classroom-like about disparate situations, there is room for sociology to try and map that underlying something. Hence this book.

The particular model presented here is drawn from the ideas of a group of authors, some sociologists and some social psychologists, who call themselves *symbolic interactionists*. This sounds formidable, but it is not difficult to understand because it embodies an approach to the study of human life very close to the way we run our ordinary lives. If you imagine yourself taking a new job in a strange milieu – say as a ward orderly in a large hospital – think how you would learn the job. Probably you would watch other orderlies, ask them about what you should be doing, and you would observe how other people expected you to behave. The other orderlies, the nurses and doctors, and possibly the patients, would all give you advice, warnings, and direct instructions. A wise novice gathers as much information as she can and uses it to become a good orderly. At first it would feel strange – like acting on stage – but gradually you would become a ward orderly for long periods of time. Every time we enter a new social situation – a job, a school, a household, or a relationship – we learn how to behave by watching and asking and listening.

At its simplest, being a symbolic interactionist means doing research like that and *not* by testing, measuring and experimenting. Of course, anyone could do research this way. It is often called *participant observation* because the observer talks to, and participates in activities with, the people she is studying. Anthropologists have always worked like this when studying exotic tribes, and it is sometimes called 'anthropological' observation, or *ethnography*. The social scientists who call themselves symbolic interactionists obviously have more in common than a research method. They share a theory, or set of theories, about how social life works, which derives in the main from G. H. Mead (Rock, 1979). The relevant aspects of these ideas will be introduced throughout the book, but these will only be a fragment of the whole. A better cross-section of symbolic interactionist writing is available in a collection edited by Manis and Meltzer (1978).

Symbolic interactionists are found both in sociology and social psychology departments, for the set of theories they espouse transcends that division. In general they study situations of face-to-face interaction rather than producing theories about whole societies, or conducting artificial experiments. Educational institutions are therefore exactly the sort of topic for an interactionist approach. However, many other schools of thought exist in sociology and psychology whose exponents consider educational institutions appropriate research topics, and so no book on the classroom could legitimately draw only on the symbolic interactionists. In fact, although the symbolic interactionists have written a good deal about education, socialization and training most of their work is not about schools (Atkinson, 1983). So this book draws on symbolic interactionist material about non-teaching situations, particularly in hospitals, and will integrate it with other educational research.

The study of classrooms is a thriving branch of educational research, which has engaged psychologists, sociologists, ling-

15

uists, social psychologists, and anthropologists in recent years. Some of the work published by specialists in all these fields will be covered in this book, and where possible their results integrated. However, integration is never easy, and is sometimes impossible, for the researchers have used different techniques and have distinct theories underlying their work which are often contradictory. Many of these differences will become apparent as the argument progresses, but a few need to be spelt out at the beginning.

The intellectual context of classroom research

When researchers from different disciplines study the same substantive topics, they either fail to recognize that the topic is the same and ignore work from other specialists, or fight for possession of the topic, such struggles being characterized by mutual bitterness and incomprehension. Both patterns can be found in the history of classroom research. In the USA classroom researchers from different disciplines have ignored, or been unaware of, work done by other specialists. For example, the anthropological collection edited by Spindler (1982) ignores sociological and psychological work; the linguist Mehan (1979) ignores sociology and anthropology. In Britain, on the other hand, the researchers wage unceasing guerilla warfare among themselves, as Chanan and Delamont (1975), McAleese and Hamilton (1978) and Hargreaves (1980) show.

In general, the details of academic disputes are of interest to no one but the participants, and this is certainly the case with classroom studies. However, one or two points about the development of the research tradition need to be made if any synthesis of the disparate results is to be attempted.

Historical background

The best-known tradition in classroom studies is American and social psychological. It stems from work done between the late thirties and mid-fifties by Anderson; Lewin, Lippitt and White; Bales; and Withall, and is carefully documented by Amidon and

Hough (1967). The approach's best known exponent is Ned Flanders, whose categories for coding classroom talk (Flanders's Interaction Analysis Categories or FIAC) are shown in Figure 5.1 (p. 116). The generic name for studies of this type is *interaction analysis*, and research done with such coding systems is now so widespread in the USA, Britain, Australia, New Zealand, India, and Western Europe that many people use 'classroom research' and 'interaction analysis' interchangeably.

In fact the interaction analysis research is only part of a wider tradition of studying classrooms by coding their events using pre-specified categories. Dunkin and Biddle (1974), Gage (1978) and McIntyre (1980) are reviews of the general approach. To understand the twenty-year history of contemporary classroom research, which grew rapidly after a seminal article by Medley and Mitzel (1963), it is useful to look first at the Flanders's Interaction Analysis tradition, and then at its successor as the most fashionable research strategy.

FIAC is the best known and most widely used interaction analysis coding system and will serve as an example of the *genre*. Figure 5.1 shows ten categories into which public talk can be classified – seven for the teacher, two for the pupils, and one residual category. In the classroom the observer makes a coding of the talk every three seconds and records them sequentially. (A forty-minute lesson can produce 800 tallies.) Once a large enough sample of public talk has been collected the codings are manipulated arithmetically and various scores computed for the teacher. Using these scores any one teacher can be compared with other teachers.

Central to interaction analysis coding schedules are notions of freedom and control. Teachers are assessed according to the limits they place on pupils' freedom of speech. The more freedom the pupils have the better the teacher's score. Good 'all-American' teachers are 'integrating' not 'dominating' (Anderson), 'democratic' not 'authoritative' (Lewin *et al.*), or, in Flanders's terms, they use 'indirect' rather than 'direct' influence.

The ideological underpinning of this research tradition is blatant – the very terminology is political. Yet adherents of the

17

approach claim it to be scientific, objective, and free from observer bias! To understand how this paradox came about it is necessary to look at interaction analysis's origins in social psychology.

The golden age of American social psychology stretched from the mid-thirties until the mid-sixties – three decades of political upheaval and ideological uncertainty. Social psychology flowered throughout the New Deal, the Second World War, the McCarthy witch-hunts, and the Cold War, and only ran into crisis in the era of turmoil over involvement in Vietnam. Implicit (and occasionally explicit) in the social-psychological research of these years are anxieties about political issues: democratic versus totalitarian government, conformity versus independent judgement, prejudice, attitude change, and political belief-systems. The arrival in America (1934) of the refugee Frankfurt School (see Jay, 1973) fleeing from Nazi Germany accentuated the concern with political questions already present in Depression-torn America. The Frankfurt School provided American social psychology with its most famous work, *The Authoritarian Personality* (Adorno *et al.*, 1950), which made an enormous impact. Published as the truth about concentration camps was emerging after the war, it showed that potential recruits for the Gestapo existed in America. The USA had its poor, badly educated, cracker whites: anti-Semitic, anti-negro, ethnocentric, rigid, dogmatic, superstitious, and with a high potentiality for Fascism.

The Frankfurt School were explicitly political, while much of the other work was only implicitly so, but the overall message of the social psychology was the same – America's strength lies in democratic leadership at group level and flexible independence for the individual. This is the context from which interaction analysis sprang, and while the underlying message is explicit in Flanders's own work, it has been largely forgotten by his disciples and devotees throughout the world.

Two main claims are made, based on the findings of interaction analysis research:

(a) that the more indirect influence the teacher uses, the more favourable are the pupils' attitudes to school work;

18

(b) the more the teacher uses indirect influence, the more the pupils learn.

The first claim is better supported by the evidence and also makes more sense intuitively. I usually refer to it as the 'warm bath theory' of teacher effectiveness. If a teacher scores highly for being indirect it means she accepts and uses the pupils' ideas and feelings rather than rejecting and criticizing them, and it does seem reasonable that pupils will be happier when accepted rather than rejected! The second claim is more dubious. It makes less intuitive sense and the research findings are less clear-cut.

American classroom research today

There was a heated debate about these two central findings in the early 1970s (Rosenshine, 1971 and Flanders, 1973), which died away as the research fashion changed. In the second half of the 1970s those involved with the systematic coding of classroom events had moved on to focus on pupils and the amount of classroom time they were actually working (Rosenshine and Berliner, 1978; Denham and Lieberman, 1980). Several projects were funded concerned with this issue of 'time on task' or 'academic engaged time'. It is tempting, if somewhat fanciful, to see the 1965–75 period of Flanders-based research on how nice teachers were as typical of a 'soft', 'caring' period of American life, and the swing towards engaged time as a research topic being the result of economic recession and the advent of 'Reganomics'. Between 1965 and 1975 teachers were urged to become indirective; since 1975 the emphasis has been on how to keep their pupils' noses to the grindstone (Doyle and Good, 1982).

Most recently, the American classroom research scene has been enthused by 'ethnographic', participant observation, methods (Popkewitz and Tabachnick, 1981; Spindler, 1982) which are the main concern of this book. This latest development may bring the American and British researchers closer than they have been for years.

Classroom research in Britain

Classroom research in Britain began to grow rapidly about eight to ten years after the American boom. The pre-specified coding scheme tradition has become firmly established, but the interaction analysis sub-tradition was never as dominant in the UK. Cautionary statements were published (Walker and Adelman, 1975a; Hamilton and Delamont, 1974), and Rosenshine's (1971) *caveat* was widely quoted. There are also differences in the intellectual context of educational enquiry in this country which affect the rate of adoption for American fashions. In particular the relative strength and independence of social psychology is very different in the two countries. In America it has much greater autonomy, and this gave American social psychologists of education a strong advantage in claiming the classroom as their research territory. In Britain, however, social psychology is a *relatively* weak discipline, particularly in education. Hence classroom research has been done mainly by psychologists and 'method' specialists (i.e. those training teachers of modern languages, geography, chemistry, etc.) with a lesser number of sociologists, linguists and anthropologists.

Interaction analysis appealed to psychologists and method specialists because of its claims to scientific standards of rigour and reliability. For psychologists trained in experimental or psychometric techniques, going to watch real human beings behaving in real situations was a big step. One might parody Neil Armstrong and call the decision to observe actual classrooms a small step for man, but a giant step for psychologists. In the past the classroom had been a 'black-box' for psychologists – extroverts went in and scores on programmed maths materials came out. Many researchers trained in orthodox psychology and writing for an audience of psychologists could only justify a decision to observe if the observations were statistically reliable and valid. If the method produced numbers susceptible to factor analysis, so much the better. Those training teachers had rather different problems. They had always been present in classrooms while supervising their students, so observation was not a radical departure for them. But their student teachers complained that orthodox educational research was irrelevant, so they had strong motivation to adopt a research tradition that was classroom-based. Because most of them lacked any formal professional qualification in educational research methods, but were writing in part for an audience of researchers, they were peculiarly vulnerable to charges of being unscientific. Thus they too were under strong pressures to stick with the objective *systematic* research techniques. While the interaction analysis research was well known in Britain, the large and the notorious projects have mostly used home-grown British systems which do not focus on the emotional climate of the classroom. Thus the ORACLE project (Galton, Simon and Croll, 1980) and the work of Neville Bennett (1976, 1980) is schedule-based, but does not use interaction analysis.

The systematic classroom observers in Britain have never lost touch with those using participant observation. In the UK educational research is still so underdeveloped, and the pressures to make it experimental so strong, that anyone doing observational research of whatever type had to be sought as an ally. An informally organized network of observers grew up which included, with the psychologists and method tutors, sociologists, linguists and anthropologists. This network began in 1969 with some twenty or so workers, but grew rapidly. British classroom research has always had an inter-disciplinary flavour, as the collections of papers by Chanan and Delamont (1975), Stubbs and Delamont (1976), McAleese and Hamilton (1978), Bennett and McNamara (1979) and Hargreaves (1980) show. The relationship between the various specialists is not an easy one, but it does exist.

Apart from the 'feuding', which is a frequent consequence of interdisciplinary involvement in the same substantive topic, the most noticeable feature of British classroom research is its neglect by sociologists of education. In 1972 Rob Walker wrote:

> The interaction of teacher and pupils within the social arena of the classroom is a central element in all educational institutions, yet it has been left largely unstudied by sociologists. British sociologists of education in particular have been

dominated by a concern with an education system that has failed to give social equality of access to different parts of the system . . . they have concentrated their attention on the analysis of inputs and outputs to different institutions, and tended to assume uniformity in the nature of the educational process.

Ten years later this comment still holds substantially true. Walker's article contained a content-analysis of two well known introductory texts, Banks (1968) and Musgrave (1965), showing how little discussion of classroom was included. Given the lack of empirical research available when those texts were compiled this brevity of discussion was probably inevitable. Much more disturbing is the lack of interest shown by sociologists more recently: for example, Karabel and Halsey (1977). It appears that, since Walker wrote, school and classroom ethnography has become a respectable thing for sociologists to do, but it has had little impact on the majority of sociologists of education. Only Olive Banks has consistently called for more sociological studies of teaching processes, and increased her coverage of them as they become available. Thus, while her first edition (1968) had only eight pages on classrooms, the third has a whole chapter (1976).

Walker (1972) suggested that 'the metaphysical basis of research on education' in Britain focuses upon 'economic and social structures' – leading researchers away from the school into the home and ultimately the class structure. He wrote 'If the crucial concept in American educational research is "authoritarianism" with social psychology playing the role of social conscience, then in Britain the crucial concept is "social class" and sociology the social conscience'. Arguments about sociology of education on these lines take us straight to the heart of the perennial controversy central to sociology itself: what should be the balance between paying attention to large-scale social processes (macro-sociology) and to face-to-face interaction and to individuals (micro-sociology). Dawe (1970) has shown just how longstanding this debate has been in sociology, and this book is no place to rehearse it. Brian Davies' (1976) volume in this series concerns itself with the debate in the sociology of education. This book concentrates on studying face-to-face interaction in schools and classrooms. Such a focus has been criticized: Giddens (1981) has grave doubts about such a shift, arguing that if

> the most vital aspects of social existence are those relating to the triviata (sic) of 'everyday life', whereby the individual shapes his phenomenal experience of social reality . . . [then it is all too easy to] rationalize a withdrawal from basic issues involved in the study of macro-structural social forms and social processes. Insofar as this is the case, we simply abandon the problems which have always been the major stimulus to the sociological imagination. (p. 15)

If it were true that an involvement in the study of everyday life precluded a consciousness of wider social issues, then the distaste expressed by some educational sociologists for interactionists' perspectives (for example see Shipman, 1972) would be more understandable. However, there seems no *necessary* reason for excluding the traditional concerns of sociology from classroom-based research studies. Indeed throughout this analysis of classroom processes reference will be made to the central concerns of educational sociology. The main strengths of the symbolic interactionist approach have been analyses of face-to-face negotiations in organizations which suit the study of classrooms and their immediate context, the school. But to fail to set such analyses against large-scale social and economic processes would make them pointless. In fact, it is precisely because the social-psychological researchers do not relate their classroom studies to the wider society that they have been criticized by more sociologically-minded authors, such as Walker (1972).

In summary, then, this book uses both sociological and social-psychological research findings to provide an understanding of classroom processes. It draws on the theoretical ideas of the symbolic interactionists, but attempts to avoid some of the pitfalls of their approach. Before embarking on the details of the analysis, the overall structure of the book is spelt out and a few points made about the sources used.

23

About this book

The analysis of classroom processes which follows is arranged in four parts, which occupy Chapters 2 to 5 of this book.

Chapter 2 introduces the basic tenets of symbolic interactionism and discusses classroom 'settings'. Thus it is about the *context* of the rest of the book: the theoretical context of my analysis and the context in which classrooms are embedded. It 'sets the stage' for what follows.

Chapters 3 and 4 form a pair. They discuss research on teachers and pupils respectively. Each chapter looks at the strengths and weaknesses of the participants' bargaining positions: what resources can they mobilize in each interaction? The attitudes and beliefs (called perspectives) of teacher and pupils are examined and related to each other. These chapters introduce the protagonists.

Chapter 5 brings teacher and pupils together again and analyses what we know about the bargaining process. It is concerned with the ways in which the participants negotiate a shared world and act towards it.

In short, Chapter 2 sets the stage, Chapters 3 and 4 introduce the characters, and in 5 the action begins – or as I have subtitled it: 'Let battle commence!'

Sources and resources

There is now a substantial body of published classroom research. For this book I have chosen published material which is sociological (rather than linguistic, anthropological or psychological), and interesting. Some of the examples are from famous books, others from more obscure works. Both this text, and the accompanying reader (Delamont, 1984), use the school and classroom studies which I find most entertaining, informative or provocative. Several approaches to the study of classrooms are neglected, particularly the sociolinguistic, ethnomethodological, and conversational analysis work (see Further reading). Throughout the book there are numerous examples from my own PhD research, and references to the ORACLE project. Both these need brief explanations.

As a postgraduate I carried out *fieldwork* in several Scottish girls' schools. The term fieldwork comes from social anthropology and is a shorthand way of referring to doing participant observation. It means studying situations by immersing oneself in them, often staying away from home, in the research milieu. The longest period of fieldwork was spent in a girls' public school I called St Luke's where I studied the fourth-year pupils and the staff who taught them, attending all their activities and collecting data by a variety of methods: participant and systematic observation, formal and informal interviews, and questionnaires. Most of the data are unpublished (Delamont, 1973) although a few papers have presented some of the findings (Delamont, 1976a, 1976b, and Atkinson and Delamont, 1976). The material is used in this book because it is substantially unpublished, offers concrete examples of several points not studied by other people, and as there is still a shortage of data on girls, is a partial corrective to the male bias of the field.

The ORACLE project was a five-year, SSRC-funded research programme based at Leicester University run by Galton and Simon (1980). Pupils were observed both in primary school and as they transferred to secondary schooling, and a variety of data was collected. I was lucky enough to be involved with the programme and some of the published findings are included in the book.

2 A working relationship

The framework for understanding classroom interaction which occupies the rest of this book is, as outlined in the first chapter, based on the ideas drawn from the symbolic interactionists. Before it is presented, some discussion of Mead's ideas on human interaction is necessary. Mead died in 1931 without publishing a single book. He is, therefore, one of those seminal authors whose disciples and pupils have been left to interpret and synthesize fragmentary writings for posterity. The clearest statement of the sociological implications can be found in Blumer (1966). Briefly, the central notion of symbolic interactionist theory is that all humans are possessed of a self, and that they are *reflexive*, or self-interacting. That, simply, means that we think about what we are doing, and what goes on inside our heads is a crucial element in how we act. This self is, incidentally, not a fixed structure, frozen by our toilet training or early conditioning, but rather a dynamic, ever-changing *process*.

Following on from this is the idea that we act according to the way we see, or construe, the world about us. This belief allows for errors. It does not imply that the world each of us constructs is necessarily well built. If our constructions, and hence our actions, are too far distant from those of others to be tolerable to them, we will be considered bad or mad, and forcibly prevented from continuing to act in accordance with them. But within broad limits we can continue to interpret and act upon the world as we see it.

Mead postulated two types of human interaction, symbolic and non-symbolic. The latter is roughly equivalent to the biological notion of a reflex action – such as pulling your hand away from extreme heat, or blinking. The vast proportion of human interaction is symbolic, which means it involves interpretation. The idea is that when two people are interacting each is constantly interpreting their own and the other's acts, and reacting, and reinterpreting, and reacting, and reinterpreting, and reacting. . . . The theory assumes that there can be joint actions, or social acts in which a number of individuals act together, sharing their construction of what is going on. Weddings, pop concerts, stag nights, football games and classroom encounters are all examples of joint actions. It should be mentioned that successful participation in joint acts depends on recognizing them – that is, construing them 'correctly' – or according to the other participants' definitions of the situation. Many classic comedies depend upon one or more participants *not* recognizing the 'normal' (i.e. everyone else's) definition. The whole plot of *She Stoops to Conquer*, for example, turns on such a misidentification – of the home as an inn, the daughter of the house as a serving maid, and so on. The hero's actions, though consistent with his constructions, are viewed by others as bizarre.

It is important when thinking of social events in this way not to lose sight of the dimension of *power*. In any area of human life some participants may have more power than others – and so may be able to enforce their definition of the situation upon others. Many symbolic interactionist studies lose sight of this reality, but it clearly makes nonsense of many social situations if the power element gets lost. For example, it is fascinating to discover how prisoners construe being in prison, but the analysis is reduced to farce if one forgets that they cannot get out, or rebel against the 'screws' without reprisals.

It is also worth pointing out the research implications of

accepting a Meadian approach to human life. It does not make research impossible, but it does necessitate changes in methods. The crux of the matter is neatly summarized by Blumer:

> in short, one would have to take the role of the actor and see the world from his standpoint. This methodological approach stands in contrast to the so-called objective approach so dominant today, namely that of viewing the actor and his action from the perspective of an outside, detached observer . . . the actor acts towards his world on the basis of how he sees it and not on the basis of how that world appears to the outside observer.

When the symbolic interactionist approach is applied to classrooms, certain consequences follow. The classroom relationship of teacher and pupils is seen as a joint act – a relationship that works, and is about doing work. The interaction is understood as the daily 'give-and-take' between teacher and pupils. The process is one of *negotiation* – an on-going process by which everyday realities of the classroom are constantly defined and redefined. Anselm Strauss (1978) is an excellent exposition of his work on negotiation. The metaphor of negotiation came from Strauss *et al.* (1964), *Psychiatric Ideologies and Institutions*.

The authors were intrigued by the ways in which complex institutions, staffed by people from a wide range of professional, semi-professional and unskilled occupations, managed to function. They studied two psychiatric hospitals, one an enormous state institution full of patients in custody; the other an expensive private clinic with an international reputation. Many different 'ideologies' informed the staffs of these hospitals, frequently in direct contradiction with each other.

The researchers identified three groups of psychiatrists: those who believed in physical intervention by drugs and electricity, the psychoanalysts, and those involved in group therapy. In addition, both hospitals had 'ordinary' doctors concerned about the patients' physical welfare, who differed wildly in their attitudes to mental illness and its treatment. At the semi-professional level were nurses – with many different levels of skill and training – social workers from various ideologically distinct backgrounds, and a variety of therapists (occupational, radiology, physio, etc.). Finally, and crucial to the day-to-day running of the wards, there were the orderlies who did most of the day-to-day work. These orderlies were also a disparate group, ranging from young male college students doing casual labour, to elderly negro women, illiterate, but with a lifetime of service in hospital to draw on. The richness and complexities of the interaction between all these groups, whose ideologies and actions are often not only mutually contradictory, but also frequently in conflict with the official rules of the hospital, occupy the main part of the book. For example, a ward orderly in charge, alone, of 200 patients, has an inevitable hostility to changes perceived by the doctor as beneficial for patients, but by the orderly as disruptive of 'good order'. Strauss and his co-workers found many examples of informal 'standing arrangements' which ran directly counter to official dogma, the most striking of which dealt with transfer between wards. In both hospitals the transfer of patients between wards was officially difficult to organize, involving paper work and doctors' *imprimatur*. In practice, ward orderlies and nurses moved patients frequently, but without bureaucratic sanction. They 'lent' each other patients. Such informal arrangements were often of long duration and Strauss argues that this type of negotiation was essential for the functioning of the hospitals.

Such a framework can, of course, be applied to schools, although the symbolic interactionists in the USA have not done so. Instead they have concentrated their educational research in higher education (Becker *et al.*, 1961 and 1968). This book uses the insights of symbolic interactionist research to study the school classroom. Basic to the framework which follows is the notion that the changing patterns of classroom life are socially constructed over time, and are constantly subject to negotiation and renegotiation.

The rest of the chapter deals with the *setting* of classroom interaction: the physical, temporal, organizational and educational context in which classrooms are embedded.

Setting the scene

Setting is used here as a broad term covering all aspects of the temporal and institutional context in which any particular classroom is to be found. The usage, which follows Strauss *et al.* (1964), could be seen as equivalent to an 'ecological' approach to the interaction (Eggleston, 1977). Thus it comprises temporal aspects of classroom interaction, the formal organization of the school, the social and educational context, and the physical surroundings in which they take place. For convenience, four subheadings will be used: temporal, physical, institutional and educational.

Temporal setting

Classrooms can only be understood when it is accepted that they are situated in time. They are never static. Traditional educational research, both inside and outside classrooms, has neglected this crucial point (see below). This is partly because setting a situation in its historical context implies change, and social science is notoriously bad at handling social change. (This is particularly true of any theory involving a *structural-functional* perspective, as the sociology of education has traditionally done.) A symbolic interactionist approach, based on the notion of humans as reflexive actors, should be able to offer a less static analysis.

Firstly, any individual classroom encounter between a teacher and class can be conceived as an intersection of pupils' *careers* and the teacher's *career*. Here the term 'career' implies not just change and promotion in the occupational structure, but refers to the broader concept of changes in personal status and identity over time. Such a usage is best known from Goffman's (1968a) 'The moral career of the mental patient' in *Asylums*. Goffman writes:

> One value of the concept of career is its two-sidedness. One side is linked to internal matters held dearly and closely, such as image of self and felt identity; the other side concerns

official position, jural relations, and style of life, and is part of a publicly accessible institutional complex. (p. 119)

Such a double-sided idea can usefully be applied to the teachers in the opening scenarios of this book: a classics teacher of twenty-five years' experience, and a student maths teacher of five weeks' experience. We can imagine that both their self-images and felt-identities and their official positions and styles of life are radically different, and that understanding these variations is one key towards grasping why their classrooms are so distinct. Paralleling this are the pupils' careers, both *ensemble* and individually. The best work on pupil careers is probably Cicourel and Kitsuse's (1968) material on academic and delinquent adolescent careers, but a similar framework can be applied to the material presented on adaptation to secondary school in Nash (1973).

Following on from this it can be argued that, given the conceptualization of classroom life as the generation of shared meanings, a temporal understanding of the development of such meanings is an essential prerequisite for the comprehension of much of what one observes in the classroom. Traditionally, classroom research has been ahistorical; an interaction analyst will, for example, sample twenty third-grade social studies classes simultaneously for two periods on a Monday morning and treat them as 'typical' bits of behaviour. Anything that cannot be understood, such as the incident which follows, will be ignored – however vital it may be to the on-going life of that class and those pupils. The problems of such an ahistorical attitude can be demonstrated by the following examples, one British, one American.

Walker and Adelman (1976) describe an incident in the following manner:

One lesson the teacher was listening to the boys read through short essays that they had written for homework on the subject of 'Prisons'. After one boy, Wilson, had finished reading out his rather obviously skimped piece of work the teacher sighed and said, rather crossly:

T: Wilson, we'll have to put you away if you don't change

31

your ways, and do your homework. Is that all you've done?

    P: Strawberries, strawberries. (Laughter)

Now at first glance this is meaningless. An observer coding with FIAC would write down '7' (teacher criticizes), followed by a '4' (teacher asks question), followed by a '9' (pupil initiation) and finally a '10' (silence or confusion) to describe the laughter. Such a string of codings, however reliable and valid, would not help anyone *understand* why such an interruption was funny. Human curiosity makes us want to know *why* everyone laughs – and so, I would argue, the social scientist needs to know too. Walker and Adelman asked subsequently why 'strawberries' was a stimulus to laughter, and were told that the teacher frequently said the pupils' work was 'like strawberries – good as far as it goes, but it doesn't last nearly long enough'.

Here a casual comment made in the past has become an integral part of the shared meaning system of the class. It can only be comprehended by seeing the relationship as developing over time. An event on a larger scale, but dealing with the same point – the importance of time – is reported by Smith and Geoffrey (1968). They chronicle an occurrence which was instigated outside the classroom they were considering, but made nonsense of events within it.

> Big City has a beautiful fall season. Indian summer . . . provides an interlude between the humidity of summer and the slush and snow of winter. The urban teacher misses most of this, for he is confined to the building. . . . Usually the teacher finds satisfaction in the stabilization of his group into a working unit. . . . At Washington school these days end abruptly, for on Friday September 27 the school shudders with the consequences of a room being closed because of falling enrolment. (p. 129)

Here the unstable population of the city centre causes a drop in the school's enrolment, so that a room is closed and a teacher has to leave. The children from that room have to be redistributed, disturbing many existing classes. Geoffrey (the teacher Smith worked with) had been teaching 35 pupils. After the reshuffle he still had twelve of his original seventh graders, augmented by one new seventh grader, but had been given 22 new sixth graders. All the best and brightest of his original class had gone. Smith and Geoffrey discuss how the latter coped with this 'October Revolution', as it became nicknamed at the school, in more detail than is relevant here. What is clear, however, is that an observer entering Geoffrey's class not knowing about the upheaval would have found many inexplicable things going on – things that could only be understood in the context of the radical shift in the composition of the group.

Leila Sussman (1977) studied two innovatory programmes at a negro school called James Weldon Johnson. This school had had, in rapid succession, a traditional white racist head, a radical progressive integrationist white head, and then a militant separatist black head. (All were men.) Understanding the fate of innovatory programmes – especially discovering which got support from the headmaster – depended on grasping the politico-historical consequences of such a bewildering selection of principals. For example, several classroom teachers wanted to use DISTAR (a programme intended to provide remedial education for negro children in particular). The negro head objected to the ideology of this programme, and to the fact that adopting it publicly in the school would be an admission that children needed remedial help, so he failed to get funding to buy the materials. Some staff bought DISTAR with their own money, others gave it up. Any classroom observer needs to know about this issue to gain insight into teacher-pupil interaction at Johnson School.

Physical setting

Three aspects of the physical setting of classroom encounters may usefully be distinguished: the location of the school, the spatial relationships between the classroom and the rest of the school, and the layout and decor of the classroom itself. The location of any particular school, be it residential suburb, isolated mining village, Hebridean island (Hamilton, 1974), or urban ghetto, will of course have important consequences for the nature of classroom interaction. Such issues are discussed in

33

another volume in this series (Eggleston, 1977). The neighbour-hood and catchment area of schools has been a topic in educational research and so is documented, unlike the other two aspects of the physical setting discussed below.

The spatial relationships between classrooms and their surrounding school can have far-reaching implications for teaching and learning. Hamilton (1973 and 1975) compared the implementation of the Scottish integrated science scheme in two comprehensive schools – 'Simpson' and 'Maxwell'. Simpson is a two-site school (with one and a half miles between the sites) serving a large, pre-war, council estate. Hamilton observed first-year pupils in the annexe where they were taught science in thirty mixed-ability groups. Although there was enough work for four full-time science staff in the annexe, in practice ten people taught there, only one of whom did not commute. Five of these teachers came over for less than six periods a week, giving eleven groups more than one teacher every week, while one had three! The ten teachers were never all in the annexe together, so could not plan their teaching. As Hamilton says, 'For some of the teachers, the only means of communication was by means of a record book kept in the preparation room in which each of them indicated the work or worksheet completed each lesson. If this was forgotten, chaos ensued'. Various consequences followed. The science course at Simpson stuck very closely to the published material, especially the worksheets, and many teacher demonstrations took place instead of the pupils doing practical work. This is not what the authors of the integrated science scheme envisaged. Furthermore, '*De facto* responsibility for integrated science at Simpson Annexe was retained by the only science teacher in residence there full time. . . . Most of his free time was spent easing the organizational work-load of the teachers who commuted from the main school'.

Thus, even this teacher, working full-time on the integrated scheme, could not spend the time and effort on original work envisaged by the scheme's planners. Finally, Hamilton makes a point about the ancillary technical staff which echoes Strauss *et al.* (1964). He records that: 'Much of the day-to-day coordination was not in the hands of this teacher but the laboratory

34

assistant . . . she held a key position. Besides being the only person who knew where everything was, she also performed the essential task of ensuring the maintenance of entries in the work diary.'

At a more fundamental level, the growth of architecturally 'open' schools can have profound effects on the on-going life of the classrooms. The most vivid account so far is Smith and Keith's (1971) study of Kensington, an elementary school housed in 'an unusual rectangular columnar, white one-storey structure that hinted at the simplicity of a Greek temple' (p. 11). This school was open-plan, carpeted, colourful, and 'as if to inspire their uniqueness, the areas were indicated by terminology as unusual as their shape: the nerve centre, the perception core, the satellite kitchen, and the laboratory suites' (p. 11). Smith and Keith analyse many aspects of school life at Kensington, but throughout the interrelationships of architectural and spatial considerations and teacher-teacher and teacher-pupil encounters are carefully mapped. Bennett (1980) is a study of open-plan primary schools in Britain.

The scenarios which began this book made considerable use of material on the layout and decor of the rooms to provide 'clues' to the interactions going on inside them. Clearly the extent to which the teacher and class can influence the arrangement of furniture and fittings, material on notice boards, and even the decoration of the room varies from school to school. Indeed, within any one school the status of any particular teacher may be deduced from the degree of control she exercises over her surroundings. At St Luke's, the girls' public school described in the opening scenario, established staff (that is, full-time teachers who had been a year or more in the school) had their own rooms. Girls moved from one teacher to the next. I found that Goffman's concept of a 'setting', from *The Presentation of Self in Everyday Life* (1971), was a useful way of conceptualizing the importance of these rooms to teacher and pupils:

First, there is the 'setting', involving furniture, decor, physical layout, and the other background items which supply the scenery and stage props for the spate of human action played out before, within, or upon it. A setting tends to stay

35

put, geographically speaking, so that those who would use a particular setting as part of their performance cannot begin their act until they have brought themselves to the appropriate place and must terminate their performance when they leave it. (pp. 32–3)

One consequence of giving established teachers their own rooms was to increase the 'marginality' of newcomers and part-time teachers. They had to teach in other people's rooms, sometimes highly inappropriate settings for their performances. The young classics teacher, Miss Odyssey, described elsewhere (Delamont, 1976a), was often forced to teach in a maths room or a kindergarten. In addition, the marginal teacher had no books, maps, tapes, or other resources around her. Everything she was likely to need had to be taken into class at the outset, which gave her less flexibility than an established staff member who could draw on the 'props' stored around her, even if she had not planned to do so.

Teachers at St Luke's had considerable leeway in organizing the decor of their rooms, and the variations which resulted often provided interesting insights into the likely course of interaction with pupils. Messages about the subject taught, and the limits of relevance, could often be 'read' from the settings teachers provided for themselves. Two pairs of examples will demonstrate the point, one from English, the other from science.

Two science teachers. At St Luke's all the science staff had their own laboratories, so no science lessons took place in ordinary classrooms. (This in itself is significant. It implies that science is important, and that it is specialized and practical.) All the labs were traditional in their basic structure, with benches, stools, sinks, gas taps and cupboards full of equipment. Within this basic set-up there was still room for individual initiatives, as shown by the following material on the physics teacher, Dr Cavendish, and the biology teacher, Mrs Linnaeus.

Mrs Linnaeus's lab is in a new wing of the school. It is light and airy, and the pupils sit at long benches across the room to write, doing experiments at side benches. These side benches carry displays and apparatus: tropical fish, stick insects, frog spawn, and stuffed Victorian animals and birds jostle for space, with dozens of pot plants and experiments 'in progress'. Mrs Linnaeus has covered the notice boards with cuttings from the serious press on biological topics: animal behaviour, the brain, evolution and pollution.

Dr Cavendish's physics lab, though equally individual, is very different. In the Edwardian part of the building, it is small, cramped, dark, and slightly stuffy. There are eight, small square benches, used for practical work and writing. The side benches are packed solid with equipment, but here it is all electrical and mechanical: wires, plugs, balances, trolley boards, ticker-tape machines and volt-meters. The smaller items of apparatus, particularly wires and plugs, are all stored in old chocolate boxes – a strangely domestic touch.

Both these rooms show idiosyncratic touches imposed on their basic, impersonal style. Mrs Linnaeus' room emphasizes *life* – animals, plants, even the sunshine, conjure up images of the natural world. In contrast, Dr Cavendish's lab is strongly inanimate – yet the electrical and the mechanical have been tamed and domesticated by their arrangement and storage.

Two English teachers. Similar insights can be gained from a comparison of two English teachers. Mrs Milton and Miss Keats were both established and had rooms which were not only theirs, but also the 'home' of a form. Mrs Milton's room had been created by taking the large alcoves off two adjoining rooms to create a new, small room between them. It is therefore cramped with twenty-five desks in it, and always slightly stuffy, as there were only two small windows high in the wall. The walls are emulsioned a pale pink, and lack any of the usual noticeboards. The resident form have compensated for this by pinning photographs all over the walls from floor to ceiling. Mrs Milton's form are about twelve years of age and their choice of wall covering reflects pre-teen preoccupations: footballers, pop singers, and fashion. Hanging among these photographs are Mrs Milton's contributions – three framed reproductions and an 'op-art' calendar.

Miss Keats has a younger form, aged nine or ten, and her room is decorated with their paintings – big, splodgy, brightly coloured animals done in poster paint on sugar paper. The room itself is of standard size, with proper windows and noticeboards, which carry articles from colour supplements on various authors and poets. In addition, Miss Keats has pinned up a long article on the Californian grape strike and boycott. This last might seem a strangely political gesture for a girls' public school, but in fact had literary connotations. While the syllabuses from Scottish Certificate of Education (SCE) exams do not prescribe set texts, one of the commonest novels one finds around the schools is *The Grapes of Wrath*.

Various points can be inferred from the physical settings just described. We can deduce that Miss Keats has higher status and probably longer service at St Luke's from her superior room. Then we might hazard guesses about different attitudes to their subjects from Miss Keats's careful collection of relevant materials, while Mrs Milton's room carries no particular subject identity. Finally, one can usefully contrast the extent to which both teachers have let their forms contribute to, or even determine, the decor, with the heavily controlled appearance of the classics teacher's room which opened the book. She too was a form mistress, but nothing in the room indicated it.

Traditionally, classroom research has not considered such aspects of classroom life to be significant. If they have been noticed at all, they merely served as 'clues' in the observer's head. More research on physical settings would be rewarding.

The one aspect of physical setting which has received attention is the arrangement of the furniture. Seating pupils in small groups round tables, rather than in rows, is frequently cited as an indication of a 'progressive' regime among primary teachers, for example. This is far too simplistic a criterion, as Galton, Simon and Croll (1980) show. There is clear evidence that a pupil's seating position in the class affects whether teachers interact with them or not. Adams and Biddle (1970), for example, showed how teachers interacted more with children in a V-shaped wedge down the middle of the room – so that those pupils at the back and sides of the room got less contact.

Findings about differential students' participation correlating with seating position are reported for higher education classrooms by Parlett (1967). It is still necessary to explore the extent to which pupils are aware of such phenomena as the attention V. If some, or all, pupils are able to influence the amount of teacher attention they receive by their choice of seating, it would be fascinating to study the criteria they used to inform their choices. We need to know much more about pupils' perceptions of the minutiae of classroom life.

The institutional setting

The term 'institutional' here refers to the classroom's background – the whole school. However, I do not propose to review the literature on formal organizations (see Davies, 1973 and 1981). For this analysis, the model proposed by Strauss *et al.* (1964) will be followed. The school is seen as organized round a set of on-going negotiations, resulting in policies which are constantly reaffirmed, altered or 'lived with'. All schools have a formal organizational structure, with official policies on a wide variety of issues: admissions, expulsions, assessment, grouping, dress and attendance. In the terms of this analysis a school which has *no* rules about pupils' clothing has a policy about dress, just as much as the school which enforces rules about 'brown shoes rather than black', or the wearing of white gloves throughout the summer. No set of formal policies, however detailed, can cover all everyday occurrences, and specific events inevitably have to be negotiated. For example, the academic performance of any specific pupil has to be considered periodically to see if it is good enough to warrant a promotion, or bad enough to make a demotion necessary, or merely adequate for the current teaching group. A pupil in trouble with the police may be expelled from one school, and treated as a routine case in another, but in either institution some discussion, and probably action, will take place.

Such negotiations may be trivial or fundamental. Hannan (1975) describes how, in an 'open' school the advent of ROSLA pupils forced the staff to reconsider many of their fundamental

39

concepts and policies. The basic tenets of the school were perceived as threatened by the 'unmotivated', and various changes in teacher behaviour were arrived at by discussion and bargaining – including the taking of registers in every lesson to show the pupils that someone cared for them. At St Luke's one such incident occurred, relatively trivial in itself, but exemplifying the need for constant definition and redefinition of situations. In one staff meeting a teacher mentioned she had received a letter which excused a pupil's absence by saying she had been taking a ballet exam. The school rules stated explicitly that driving tests were not a sufficient reason for absence, and discussion ensued as to whether a ballet exam was like a driving test or like a music exam (which would have been a legitimate academic excuse). In the Orthodox Jewish school studied by Bullivant (1978) a similar negotiation was observed. All the Jewish males in school wore a *yarmelkeh* or a hat or both all the time. As Bullivant says:

> At first (it) is a novel sight, especially in the classroom when confronted by pupils still wearing caps . . . it soon loses its unfamiliarity until the sight of a boy *not* wearing (one) prompts one's automatic reminder to him to cover his head properly. (pp. 48–9)

The principal's insistence on pupils wearing a *yarmelkeh* was total: 'On one occasion during a staff meeting, he was asked by the gentile sports master to permit boys to remove their caps or *yarmelkehs* while tumbling on mats during gym periods.' He thought about this, and ruled that instead boys must pin their head covering to their hair and keep their heads covered even in the gym. Such reworkings of shared meanings are an essential part of any formal organization, including schools.

Institutional control

All schools have a set of rules and policies concerning the pupils' conduct – the sphere of discipline or *institutional control*. However, the extent and nature of the institutional control system varies from school to school, as does the extent to which the school regime penetrates into the classroom. Lambert *et al.* (1970) developed measures of institutional control to differentiate boys' and mixed boarding schools, which Wober (1971) adapted for girls' boarding schools. However, neither study mentions the relationship between organizational regimes and classroom climate – a criticism equally applicable to the comparative study of organizational factors in secondary schools by King (1973). The argument here only concerns the penetration of the school's wider control system into the teacher's private domain, in ways such as those discussed by Metz's (1978) *Classrooms and Corridors*. Metz, comparing two American junior high schools, suggests that there was a relationship between order in the wider school and classroom activity. She says that at Hamilton School the public (e.g. corridor, yard and cloakroom) behaviour of pupils was 'noisy and boisterous' (p. 185). Individual staff could 'see' that the whole school had a 'law and order' problem, and all were forced to examine ways of tackling it throughout the school. At Chauncey, where public control was tight, teachers with classroom difficulties saw them as private problems, and hesitated to discuss student indiscipline. Staff were ignorant of the amount of disorder in the classes of their colleagues, and saw discipline as an individual problem for each teacher to struggle with.

As I have outlined earlier, the development of 'open' schools is undermining the distinction between the classroom – the teacher's private domain where a personal 'rule of thumb' authority system can prevail – and the public arena of the wider school where behaviour is visible, and a more universalistic system of authority is apparent. However, most schools still have classrooms with four walls and a door, and so the distinction between authority systems is still a useful one. If we separate three aspects of the teacher's role, custodial, bureaucratic, and 'knowledge imparting', it is clear that the two former are usually visible to colleagues while the third is not. All three aspects can be relevant when studying classroom interaction, but only the first two are normally important in the wider organization. Leading on from this, we can argue, following Becker (1953), that the individual teacher's support of the 'authority system' is the crucial element in her relationships with colleagues. In contrast, the academic content of the teacher-pupil relationship is generally invisible and non-accountable.

Understanding the relationship between the authority system and educational concerns is difficult, precisely because of their concentration in different spheres. There is very little systematic research into the links between arenas. Sussman's (1977) findings about the fate of DISTAR in the ghetto school described above are one such example of how the power disparity between head and classroom teachers can affect the curriculum. Bullivant's (1978) work in the Orthodox Jewish school is focused on the religious authority system and its relation to the academic curriculum. Bullivant found the Jewish authority system focused on the rabbis working in the school was much more powerful than the secular, academic curricular system. Ann Swidler (1979) has studied the effects at classroom level of working in high schools which were officially 'free' schools. She found that the official policies of student 'freedom' embodied in the two schools observed had clear consequences for classroom life. The teachers had renounced conventional teacher authority, and Swidler documents how this affected the curriculum and teacher-pupil relations. Pupils expected to decide what they would 'learn' and teachers had to rely on individualized appeals to shared human values. In general, though, we lack detailed studies of the school regime/classroom interaction interface. The theoretical model for such an exploration is, however, present in Bernstein's (1971) classic paper on educational knowledge.

Classification and framing. Bernstein's paper puts forward two dimensions for the analysis of educational systems – classification and frame. Classification refers to the boundary kept between academic subjects, the degree to which they are kept separate or allowed to mingle. Strong classification characterizes a school like St Luke's, where history and English are taught as completely unrelated subjects – so much so that during my fieldwork the history department were teaching my sample the

42

French Revolution and one English teacher was reading *A Tale of Two Cities* with the same class, and yet none of them knew what the others were doing, or utilized the knowledge when I mentioned it to them. Weak classification characterizes a school where pupils work on topic or projects using materials of a literary, historical, sociological, scientific, or artistic nature as they choose. *Frame* is a more difficult idea to grasp, but refers to the degree of control over what can be taught, and how and when it is to be taught, which is vested in the teacher and pupils. Strong framing is exemplified by programmed learning, weak framing by a 'free' class in which pupils choose what they will 'learn' and how to 'learn' it.

In Bernstein's original paper these concepts are used to differentiate types of secondary and tertiary education across countries – that is, at a macro-level. They are not grounded in the school or the classroom, although it is at these levels that I want to use them here. Just as schools can be differentiated according to the nature and extent of their institutional control systems, so too can they be characterized by the strengths of the classification and framing of educational knowledge they embody. Such a characterization can then be related to other organizational aspects – and thus the institutional setting linked to the educational setting.

The educational setting

The classroom has to be seen against a background of an educational system operating at school, local and national levels. At the school level, with which we are here concerned, educational policies are subject to constant bargaining, like the organizational system. Educational policies relate to such issues as the choice of curricula, forms of assessment, provision of appropriate texts and other resources, and 'proper' qualifications for staff recruits. All such policies must be understood in relation to the school's location in a grid of classifications and frames, pertaining to all subjects included in the school's work.

Some specific examples illustrate these points. As stated above, Bernstein did not locate his concepts in schools or classrooms – yet it is precisely in the differences in strengths of the classification and frame at the various levels of organization that continuous negotiations become apparent. The strength of the classification and frame is not constant across them. The Scottish Certificate of Education (SCE) examinations in English at ordinary and higher grade do not prescribe set texts for study. Teachers are free to choose what novels, plays and poems they read with their classes. This looks like an example of weak framing, and at the level of official, national policy, it is. However, at school level, a head of English may well prescribe what books other teachers use – giving strong framing for the majority of teachers. Alternatively, a head of department may leave the teachers free, and in any particular classroom the teacher may leave the pupils to choose what they want to study, giving them exceptionally weak framing. Understanding what is going on in any specific classroom may be dependent on knowing about all these three levels – national, institutional, and individual.

However, even this sub-division of framing, locating it at various levels, is not subtle enough. It is still necessary to distinguish between the *hidden* and *manifest* aspects of the knowledge code. Every syllabus and curriculum has, in addition to its public, official specifications (the manifest curriculum) its unspecified, taken-for-granted 'rules', which also have to be mastered – the hidden curriculum (see Snyder, 1971, and Becker *et al.*, 1961 and 1968). The SCE English exams will serve to illustrate this point. The manifest curriculum does not specify any particular authors or texts, but visits to schools show many classes studying the same few authors – Shakespeare, Chaucer, Dunbar and Burns – and the same handful of novels are read by pupils in dozens of schools (*The Heart of the Matter, The Grapes of Wrath, Animal Farm, The Heart of Darkness, Lord of the Flies*). The hidden curriculum appeared to specify a small group of set texts, quite contrary to the manifest one. In part, of course, this can be 'explained' by money – schools have to use books they have in stock. The teachers, however, explain it differently. They see themselves as constrained by the universities. Teacher after teacher argued that it would not be fair to pupils if they went to university, where they would be expected to read Shakespeare and Chaucer unaided, if they had not learnt how to study them in school. (The 'truth' of this belief is, of course, irrelevant; the important 'fact' is the teacher's conviction.) Here the manifest curriculum shows weak framing, while the hidden curriculum exhibits strong framing.

The concept of classification needs to be seen in a similar way – that is potentially varying in strength at different organizational levels of the education system and between the hidden and manifest curricula. The Scottish Integrated Science scheme discussed by Hamilton (1975) will serve as an example. At national level, the official publications specify an integrated approach to science to be taught to mixed ability groups for the first two years of secondary education. Physics, chemistry and biology should disappear as separate subjects at this level, and science should be taught round topics, such as energy. At national level, this is clearly an attempt to implement a weakening of the boundaries between sciences – i.e. a weak classification. However, as Hamilton shows, at school level the formal organizational structure still embodied strong classification; the schools had separate subject departments for physics, chemistry and biology, staffed by specialists whose allegiances were to those departments first of all. At classroom level Hamilton found the teaching very dependent on the published worksheets, for reasons discussed above, and so the classification was weaker than at school level – though far from that envisaged by curriculum planners. Here, the official, manifest curriculum embodies weak classification, but Hamilton's study of the hidden curriculum shows strong classification predominating.

An evaluation of Individually Guided Education (IGE) in the USA by Popkewitz *et al.* (1982) shows that the 'in-school' fate of an educational innovation is heavily dependent on the school it is introduced to. The IGE programme worked in the way its inventors planned in wealthy suburban elementary schools, but in two ghetto schools the existing school dynamics conquered the innovation which was conscripted into their value system.

In this chapter I have argued that classroom processes can only be *understood* if their context is understood. This means

45

studying their location in time and space, and comprehending the organizational and educational background in which they are embedded. Only when these features of classroom life have been analysed – when the stage setting has been researched – can the investigator hope to understand the events which occur behind the classroom door. The next two chapters introduce the protagonists: the teacher and the pupils.

3   The protagonists: the teacher

Chapter 2 set the scene for classroom interaction. This chapter concentrates on one of the protagonists, the teacher, and forms a pair with Chapter 4, in which the focus shifts to the pupils. Of course, separating teacher and pupils in this way is highly artificial, in that neither could exist without the other, but their roles, power and perspectives are *so* different it seems clearest to separate them. They are, of course, reunited in Chapter 5!

The teacher's role

If I tell you that Mrs Smith is the head of history at St Trinian's, you can distinguish three separate bits of information about her. Mrs Smith is an individual, a member of the teaching profession, and she holds a specific post at St Trinian's. If she left St Trinian's she would still be a teacher. If she became the school counsellor she would cease to be a teacher but would still belong to St Trinian's. When discussing teachers we have to separate out the attributes of the occupation – teaching – from the attributes of a specific post – at St Trinian's – from the characteristics of any individual person.

Teaching is a job, but in becoming a teacher one learns to

occupy a *role*. Role is a key concept in social science, discussed most succinctly by Brown (1965), who says of it: 'The word *role* is borrowed from the theatre and there is little in its social-psychological sense that is not prefigured in its theatrical sense' (p. 152). Thus, just as the role of Hedda Gabler has existed for over fifty years, and been played by many actresses, so too the role of teacher has existed for centuries and many different people have been teachers. Roles prescribe certain ways of behaving, but also allow an amount of 'creative interpretation'. Brown suggests that, for example:

> A college president must meet with the trustees, supervise the administrative staff, and try to raise funds . . . but in his public addresses he is free to stress scholarship, football, or the 'whole man'. (p. 153)

We must augment this, to add institutional variation, and point out that one college president may have to speak Latin on degree day, and another Welsh, but both would still have to supervise their staff and be free to emphasize scholarship or sport in their speeches. In any discussion of teachers we must examine the attributes common to all teachers and be sensitive to institutional and personal variations.

All teachers come to the classroom with certain bargaining counters and certain attitudes in common, because they are teachers. Against this, because teaching is a highly segmented occupation, there are deep cleavages between different branches of the profession. These may be based on the level of school in which teaching is done (nursery, primary, grammar, FE); the level of professional qualification (graduate versus non-graduate, honours versus ordinary graduates, trained versus untrained); and the relative status of the education sector in which they work (state, direct grant, independent). At primary schools hostility may exist between graduate and certificated staff – particularly when the former draw larger salaries for doing the same job. At secondary level the old tripartite system separated graduates (in the grammar, direct grant and public schools) from non-graduates (in secondary modern schools). Comprehensive reorganization brings the two together in the same school, and into competition for the same posts. Differences in attitude between teachers emphasizing the academic and the pastoral aspects of their jobs are now institutionalized with the development of separate academic and pastoral structures (Hannan, 1975; Richardson, 1973).

Thus, although the non-graduate nursery school teacher *is* a member of the same occupational group as a graduate maths master at Eton, they cannot be expected to share many attributes and attitudes, or have similar life styles. Yet their everyday classroom life is similar. Just as the three classrooms described in Chapter 1 were different and yet the same, so too those three teachers were doing something recognizably the same – teaching. It is this sameness which this book aims to draw out.

Clearly there are dozens of things that can be said about teachers and their role – whole books have been written about the profession. However, most of the research has not considered classroom behaviour at all. For example, we know a good deal about teacher militancy, but nothing about how teachers who believe in strike action differ, in the classroom, from those who think striking unprofessional – if indeed they do. This means that our knowledge about 'the teaching profession' is totally divorced from our knowledge about job performance. Therefore, for this book, I am forced to use most of the extant research as a background from which a few themes relating to classroom interaction can be drawn.

Immediacy and autonomy

The first two themes come from Jackson's (1968) *Life in Classrooms*, one of the most stimulating books in education. Jackson suggests various themes which capture the essential nature of teaching, two of which are *immediacy* and *autonomy*. In the introduction I contrasted the privacy of the conventional classroom with the more complex relationships of the 'open' variety. I said that the first two teachers were 'in the best and worst senses of the term, on their own'. This privacy is closely interrelated with immediacy and autonomy – the three

49

are interdependent. The immediacy stems partly from the large number of pupils confronting the teacher. Nothing never happens. To quote Jackson, 'there is a here-and-now urgency and a spontaneous quality that brings excitement and variety to the teacher's work . . .' (pp. 119–20). Quantitative studies of classrooms show that the teachers may be engaging in a thousand interpersonal exchanges every day! This urgency means that many of the teacher's decisions have to be immediate. There is little chance to reflect and none to get a 'second opinion'. This is radically different from the doctor or lawyer. Even the busy GP with a stream of patients can ask her partner, or send the patient to hospital for a second opinion, or ask for tests, before diagnosing or prescribing. Solicitors too have partners, law books, and barristers to consult. The teacher's professional colleagues are out of reach, and only long-standing problems, or crises, can be looked up in text books, or referred to colleagues. Immediacy and privacy are closely related as Andrew Pollard (1980) has shown in studies of British primary teachers.

Allied to privacy and immediacy is autonomy. The teacher is alone and in control. She has power or authority over many aspects of pupils' lives: knowledge, behaviour, speech and clothing all come within her sphere of control. Seeing the teacher in terms of her control over pupils brings power into the centre of the analysis. As I have already pointed out, the symbolic interaction approach has been criticized for neglecting power. When using an interactionist framework it is easy to become so enamoured of, for example, the drug-takers' world view, that one forgets the legal power and social reinforcement behind the policeman's social construction of drug abuse. Few negotiations are between equal partners, and classrooms are no exception. Teacher and pupils come to the classroom in very different bargaining positions.

Control over knowledge

The teacher's most potent resource is her possession of, access to, and control over knowledge. She has knowledge and she defines what should and what should not be learnt, albeit within the educational context (i.e. the classification and framing system) outlined in Chapter 2. In one way, saying that the teacher controls knowledge seems trite. We all expect a teacher to know more than her pupils – we take it for granted. However, because we assume it we do not always recognize the ways in which it is constantly reaffirmed in everyday classroom life. Consider the following incident from a lesson on the history of the Napoleonic wars which followed material on British politicians of the period. As soon as the whole group had assembled:

> Evelyn puts up her hand. Mrs Flodden acknowledges it, and asks what she wants.
> Evelyn: I've got an epigram about Burke – can I read it?
> Mrs F. says yes 'of course'. Evelyn reads her epigram and gets laughter from the class.
> Mrs F. gets Evelyn to write it on the board so anyone who chooses can copy it down. Then announces 'notes on the Napoleonic wars'.

This is an ordinary classroom exchange which, at first glance, has no features worthy of comment. However, it shows, as almost every other exchange shows, who really controls lesson content. As the lesson opens Evelyn makes a contribution relevant to the previous lesson. She offers an epigram. Note that by *offering* it, she implies she has no natural right to teach the class, she asks permission. (We can assume that, because Evelyn feels confident enough to offer her epigram, Mrs Flodden is likely to accept it – not all teachers receive such offers.) Mrs Flodden grants her the privilege – and then immediately 'colonizes' it. She tells Evelyn to put the verse on the board, and so defines it as a piece of information that can be officially recorded. It is not, however, so important that writing it down is compulsory in the way the notes on the Napoleonic wars are. By implication, therefore, Mrs Flodden defines the epigram as marginal to history, the notes central.

This is, in part, an aspect of the distinction drawn in Chapter 2 between the hidden and the manifest curriculum. The hidden curriculum is not publicly accountable, and so, although the teacher controls both aspects, her power over the manifest curriculum is not so great. Teachers are constantly defining and redefining the limits of the hidden curriculum, implicitly showing pupils what is 'really' relevant and important. Keddie (1971) presents an extract from a lesson on sex roles and the division of labour, based on materials which are designed to suggest that traditional roles and stereotypes are cultural, not biological, and hence open to discussion.

> Teacher: No [women] feel the same pain, but they have a greater resistance to it.
> Boy: What are they always crying for?
> Teacher: Well, that's temperament, isn't it? Anyway, we're getting away from the point about the Eskimos, aren't we?

Here the teacher defines as irrelevant a pupil question which, to an outsider reading the transcript, looks like a perfect example of what the social science syllabus ought to be producing. Science lessons can produce similar interactions, as Young (1976) has shown:

> Teacher: It will be what you call the pea shoot so you've got/
> Boy 1: What kind of pea is it?
> Boy 2: It's just an ordinary/
> Teacher: It's a dried pea, probably a dried pea that you buy in a shop.

In this example a West Indian pupil raises a question about varieties of pea, which is certainly relevant to biology – the taxonomy of pea sub-species. However, the teacher does not accept that pea classification, 'a pervasive feature of the folk biology of West Indian culture', is part of school science. In both extracts the teacher's definition of what knowledge is appropriate to the lesson is paramount, unexamined, and undefended.

The pupils studied by Keddie and Young were working class, school 'failures'. Bullivant (1978) teaching in an Orthodox Jewish school reports how the academic scientific curriculum was constantly challenged by the boys because it went against their Judaic beliefs. He says (1978):

> On several occasions with my fifth form a geography lesson would touch on an aspect of geology and the age of rocks. 'The

Silurian rocks in this region were laid down some 400 million years ago', I would state, only to have one or the other of the most Orthodox boys challenge the statement. 'This cannot be. In *Chumash* it says the world was created 5729 years ago' . . . 'We know the truth . . . because Moses has given it to us.' (p. 147)

Bullivant shows how hard life was for gentile teachers in the school, because they were always in possession of less powerful knowledge than the rabbis.

Keddie and Young demonstrate the relationship between control over lesson content and the privacy and immediacy of classroom life. In both extracts teachers are 'put on the spot' by pupils' questions which demand quick, 'off-the-cuff' answers if the pace and direction of the lesson are to be sustained. Both teachers might well, on reading the transcripts, wish they had behaved differently – but in the absence of colleagues, in the press of classroom events, we all cut off promising questions and rush on with our definitions of relevance.

Vulnerability

Paradoxically, as hinted above, the privacy, immediacy, and autonomy of the teacher's working life are both potent resources, and vulnerable points in their defence systems. If control of content is the teacher's strongest resource, it is also her Achilles' heel. Threats to the control over knowledge disturb teachers at all levels of the education system from infant school to university, as studies both of conventional instruction and curriculum development projects have shown. Philip Jackson's (1968) interviews with outstanding teachers show them reacting violently to threats aimed at their curricular autonomy:

A fourth-grade teacher with a decade of experience was equally adamant when asked to consider the possibility of increased restrictions in her choice of teaching materials. She first blurted out, 'I'd get fired! I wouldn't do it!'

Bellack and his collaborators (1966) inadvertently highlighted this vulnerability while studying economics instruction in American high schools. They were trying to apply some ideas derived from Wittgenstein to classroom discourse and wanted tape recordings of lessons for linguistic analysis. Their idea was to standardize the *content* of the lessons to concentrate upon teaching style and language use. Accordingly, Bellack found volunteers who were prepared to base four lessons on a pamphlet about international trade supplied by the research team. The pupils' grasp of the material supplied was to form part of the research data. Bellack and his collaborators thought, therefore, that they would be able to study a range of teaching techniques (the volunteers were told to teach the material in any way they liked) applied to an identical body of content. In fact, quite the reverse occurred. Bellack's results show that the teachers' styles were statistically very similar but, 'although teachers . . . were unequivocally directed and limited in the subject matter to be covered . . . the data for the substantive meanings covered in the classroom reveal the greatest variability among [them]' (p. 68). Each class had a unique pattern of content coverage. The most striking feature was the variety in dealing with free trade, ostensibly the subject of the pamphlet. In theory this was the central focus of all the classes, but some concentrated instead on trade barriers, and some on generalized discussions of trade. In short, the teachers were extremely cavalier in their treatment of the pamphlet, and Bellack is forced to admit that his research team failed dismally to standardize lesson content. This failure spoilt their experimental design, but is a nice illustration of my argument about control of content being a source of power and weakness. With the best will in the world, teachers cannot, or will not, relinquish it.

The point can be illustrated further by reference to studies of curriculum developments which have tried to change the traditional relationship between teacher and knowledge base. The 'Nuffield' approach to science teaching, which emphasized guided discovery rather than lecturing and demonstrating, was one such initiative. Hailed as revolutionary, Nuffield science was thought to be sweeping the schools. In fact, while the manifest curricula have changed as exam syllabuses incorporate

Nuffield ideas, the hidden curriculum, of classroom life, has changed little. In a large-scale, official evaluation of new science teaching, Galton and his co-workers observed over 100 teachers all over England in over 300 lessons. They found little evidence of the new techniques. A quarter of their sample never asked pupils to plan the design of experiments, and only seventeen teachers were operating in the true 'Nuffield' manner (Eggleston, Galton and Jones, 1976).

The Nuffield science curricula demanded a shift in the teacher's role from lecturer/demonstrator to the stage manager of guided discovery processes. The Schools Council Humanities Curriculum Project (HCP) asked its teacher to make an even more dramatic change. From being the source of knowledge, the teacher was to become a neutral chairperson. The HCP was designed to teach humanities to ROSLA pupils by means of discussion groups on controversial issues. These small groups were to be chaired by the teacher, but her role was to be closer to that of David Jacobs in *Any Questions* than to any conventional classroom function. A diversity of social and political views was to be encouraged. To preserve the chairperson's neutrality the pupils' information came from the materials provided by the central course team.

It is clear from the project reports that many of the teachers involved found this new role distasteful or impossible. Press coverage of the HCP produced correspondence showing that many other teachers in Britain had reservations about the role change. Many reasons can be suggested for the project's difficulties, but its director Stenhouse (1973) locates its central problem in the area of control. Control over knowledge and control over conduct were revealed as inextricably linked:

> The problem we were tackling, and the way it was tackled, did not make a direct contribution to problems of discipline and control. In some ways it made these problems more acute. It opened them up instead of containing them, and thus ran counter to the hopes of many teachers. (p. 157)

In several ways the reports of the HCP in action have parallels with 'lessons' in the free schools studied by Swidler (1979).

There teacher control of content and of pupil behaviour were found to be inextricably linked.

Control over pupils

Stenhouse's conclusion leads us neatly into a consideration of the other consequences of teacher autonomy and privacy: control over pupil speech, behaviour and clothing. Teachers have the right to monitor and correct pupils' talk in ways that differ sharply from the norms of everyday conversation (see Stubbs, 1983 in this series). Consider the following extract from Stubbs (1975):

> Teacher: . . . but how would you be speaking – to a person you were telling off – Renaud – about time I heard your voice this morning – so wake up – it's not very difficult Renaud, this – for even you – come on Renaud – show some sparks of life . . . suppose I am telling you off – how would I be speaking to you . . . do you understand or have you been lost by the wayside somewhere . . . do you understand what I am saying – well, then, come on . . . we're all waiting Renaud . . . it's not very difficult this . . . well for example, would I be speaking to you very sweetly – if I were telling you off – in a very friendly way . . . what – pardon?
>
> Pupil: No.
>
> Teacher: Well speak up – don't speak to your hand – your hand is not very interested in this – we are – again . . .
>
> Pupil: No.

Note the typical teacher utterances: 'about time I heard your voice this morning' and 'well speak up – don't speak to your hand'. Neither of these would be acceptable in ordinary conversation, yet both seem quite natural when a teacher says them. Any teacher can tell a pupil to repeat something, rephrase it, say it in a foreign language, make it louder or softer, put it into correct English, or negate it altogether. Normally these would be peculiar. Imagine you met me at a party and asked after the local cricket team. You would find it strange if I answered 'speak up so everyone can hear!', 'answer the question!', or 'right, now say that in French!' Yet teachers say that sort of thing all the time. Monitoring and correcting pupil talk is part of the teacher's job.

Teachers are also expected to monitor and correct pupils' behaviour. Sanctions range from physical violence through systematic humiliation (see Woods, 1979) to the more sinister techniques of behaviour modification. Discussion about punishment in schools always turns on what sanctions teachers should be allowed – their right to *some* power over pupils' behaviour is not questioned. Because of the rapidity of classroom events teachers have to make decisions about whether or not to correct pupils' behaviour and speech hundreds of times every day. Each decision will be affected by many factors, but one important one will be location. As I argued in Chapter 2, we need to distinguish the privacy of the classroom, with its 'rule-of-thumb' authority system, from the wider school, where a more universalistic standard applies. Within the classroom a teacher can operate an idiosyncratic system of control. For example, Moody (1968) found that in a girls' secondary modern school she had developed a classroom regime totally different from that of her colleagues. The school regime was strict and petty. As Moody saw it:

> There was the teacher in the habit of stopping girls with short skirts and unravelling them herself, at the waist – in public. There was the ban on jewellery because, as one teacher explained, it looked 'cheap'. Maybe it was – cheaper than hers. There was the continual nagging about uniform. And the preoccupation with makeup.

Moody only gradually came to realize that this school regime existed and when she asked which staff enforced the rules she was told 'all of them 'cept you'. Such isolation is only possible because of classroom privacy and autonomy – and yet because of them a teacher can, like Moody, become dislocated from the rest of the staff. Such dislocation from the main body of the staff can have serious implications, as in Woods's (1979) account of a misfit teacher he calls David Sylvester, who eventually resigned from Lowfield School because his classroom 'standards' were unacceptable to the head. Sylvester did not share the general staffroom view of the head, and could draw little support from his colleagues. For, although the teacher's colleagues are not available for consultation all the time, they are one of the ways in which some of the disadvantages of privacy and autonomy can be mitigated.

The teacher's friends

Unfortunately we are very short of data on the professional relevance of teachers' friendship networks. Hargreaves (1972) contains an entertaining chapter on staffroom relationships. He contrasts the formal hierarchy of the organization with the informal relationships of the staffroom, and writes amusingly of the latter:

> I know of one school where one staffroom was entirely given over at lunchtime to those teachers who enjoy crosswords; in turn the clues to the crossword in *The Times*, *The Guardian*, and *The Daily Telegraph* were publicly read out to an enthusiastic audience. My presence was ignored until I managed to solve a fairly difficult clue. (p. 403)

Hargreaves goes on to suggest some of the attitudinal differences which may divide staffroom cliques: school politics (streamers versus mixed-ability-groupers), national party politics (Labour versus Conservative), religion (non-Catholics in a Catholic school), educational controversies ('progressives' versus 'traditionalists'). Groups may also form round differences in sex, age, experience, subject taught, smoking, running school drama, and so on. Sometimes these divisions are accentuated by formal or informal organizational arrangements. Scottish secondary schools often have a men-only staffroom as well as a mixed one. At many schools there are sub-groups of subject teachers who brew their own tea and avoid the main staffroom.

Hargreaves's account of such divisions is entertaining, but lacks two important dimensions. He does not mention that the divisions within the staffroom often reflect the deep cleavages which divide the teaching profession, and are thus more fundamental than he suggests. Hargreaves also fails to discuss how teachers' friends affect classroom teaching, except as a means of confirming pupil reputations (which I discuss below). Friendship is an important classroom resource, though we know little about it. The topic is mentioned by Peterson (1964), but the best example is to be found in Smith and Geoffrey (1968).

Using one's friends

Geoffrey had a strong clique of friends in the school with whom he drank coffee and shared educational ideas. After the room closure (discussed in Chapter 2), he was faced with a class of mixed ages and abilities, which he had great difficulty in teaching. His problems were ameliorated by an informal arrangement with another teacher: 'After a month with the split level classes, Mr Geoffrey and Miss Norton began discussions of trading pupils for more homogeneous grouping' (p. 166). Eventually Geoffrey took a large number of the more advanced students while Norton took the 'kooks' for more elementary work. This trading of pupils mirrors the swapping of mental patients by ward staff described by Strauss (1964). Geoffrey and Norton swapping pupils is a good example of an informal standing arrangement running counter to official policy, so characteristic of complex institutions. It also shows how a teacher's friends can lessen the difficulties of autonomy and privacy by practical help.

Reference groups

Apart from such practical help, the teacher's colleagues are a central element in her classroom performance because they form the *reference group* which determines her *perspectives*. How a teacher thinks about the classroom – her social construction of it – is a crucial element in what she does. Both perspective and reference group are important concepts in symbolic interactionist theory and have a range of meanings attached to them. Here I am following Shibutani (1955), who defines perspective to mean something similar to the conventional notion of attitude:

> A perspective is an ordered view of one's world – what is taken for granted about the attributes of various objects, events and human nature. The fact that men have such ordered perspectives enables them to conceive of their changing world as relatively stable, orderly and predictable.

Thus a perspective is an ordered set of beliefs and orientations within which, or by reference to which, situations are defined and construed by teachers (and pupils). Symbolic interactionists use the term perspective in conjunction with the idea of the reference group. This term is common in social psychology, but again following Shibutani:

> A reference group, then, is that group whose outlook is used by the actor as the frame of reference in the organization of his perceptual field. All kinds of groupings . . . may become reference groups. Of greatest importance for most people are those groups in which they participate directly. . . . But in some transactions one may assume the perspective attributed to some social category – a social class, an ethnic group, those in a given community, or those concerned with some special interest. (pp. 163–4)

For the teacher, then, one reference group is likely to be all her colleagues, or some sub-group of them. Where this is not so, as with Moody (1968), severe problems can arise. If we compare Smith and Geoffrey (1968) with Kozol's (1967) account of teaching in the Boston ghetto, this shows up clearly. Kozol is obviously alienated from all his colleagues – they are not a reference group for him, and their perspectives are not his. Where Geoffrey is a successful ghetto teacher, Kozol's position becomes untenable and he is removed. He had clearly violated what Becker (1953) emphasizes as the crucial element in maintaining colleague relationships – sharing their perspectives on the authority system and enforcing it.

Two sets of researchers have looked at how staff who teach the same subject may share a sub-culture and form a reference group. Ball and Lacey (1980) looked at the English departments in four comprehensive schools, while Gleeson and Mardle (1980) researched two subject departments (Mining and Liberal Studies) in an FE college. The English teachers across the four schools experienced English teaching rather differently according to the strength of their department within their school, and the shared perspectives of that department. Gleeson and Mardle found that the Mining staff in the FE college studied were closely identified with the mining industry and had adopted an 'industrial' frame of reference. The Liberal Studies department was less united, and there were three groups of staff within it, which Gleeson and Mardle (pp. 106–7) termed 'liberals', 'radicals', and 'cowboys'. The 'liberals' were the best-established members of the department who held a traditional view of the 'civilizing' function of the subject. The 'radicals' regarded liberal studies as bourgeois ideology and themselves as challenging its orthodoxy, but taught the approved syllabus. The 'cowboys' rejected the college syllabus and wanted to 'entertain' students or allow spontaneity and student-choice of syllabus. In the college studied, the senior, liberal group was dominant, but each teacher clique was a reference group for its adherents.

Of course, teachers may have reference groups outside their own school which are relevant to their perspectives on their job within it. For example, teachers of English, science, and so on, may belong to specialist subject associations, or be involved in curriculum projects, or sit on CSE panels, while head teachers may look to other principals, and so forth. In addition all teachers will have reference groups outside education, such as their ethnic group, political party or the WLM, and these may give them perspectives on their day-to-day work. However, in their everyday activities, perspectives shared with, and generated by, reference groups within education are usually the most important.

'Sizing up' pupils

Teachers spend a great deal of time thinking and talking about pupils. This is not idle gossip, but an essential part of their

61

teaching activities. For the teacher to act towards the pupil she must have some conception of him or her – some expectations of what the pupil will do and say. Teachers' perspectives on pupils are a crucial element in classroom interaction, and they must spend time 'sizing up' pupils.

Teachers are constantly engaged in the social construction of their pupils. The 'rules' by which such social constructions are assembled among the staff come from two sources: professional training and 'experience'. Members of all professions have these two sources for their occupational perspectives: the body of professional knowledge acquired during training and their own experience gained on the job. The doctor, for example, has her anatomy, physiology, pathology, and so on, and her experience of handling patients and recognizing illness in practice. Similarly, the teacher has a series of more or less systematic theories about education derived from her training, and a set of *ad hoc* beliefs about practice derived from her years at the 'chalk face' and the 'folk wisdom' of her reference groups. Of course, whereas it is generally accepted that medical knowledge is scientific, educational theory is not. The educational sciences are based on a mixture of imprecise social science (usually badly taught to an unwilling audience) and 'tips for teachers' garnered from great educators of the past and current lecturers in education. Thus whereas it is conceivable that elements in the doctor's perceptions of patients and their illness can be separated and traced back to either medical science or 'experience', the teacher's social construction of pupils is more muddled and cannot be disentangled so easily.

A comparison of Becker's (1953) and Jackson's (1968) analysis of interviews with Chicago teachers shows this muddle, and reveals a paradox. Becker emphasizes the teachers' stereotyped judgements about upper- and lower-class children: 'Here the children come from wealthy homes. That's not so good either. They're not used to doing work at home', and 'They never heard of a toothbrush or going to a dentist'. Jackson, on the other hand, stresses the teachers' concentration on individual children: 'Take Billy, for instance'; 'The little girl whose drawing I just described'; and 'One of those youngsters is a PhD and is on the Faculty of —— now' (pp. 139–41).

Thus two separate dimensions in the teacher's perspectives on pupils can be distinguished: the theoretical versus the practical, and the stereotypical versus the idiosyncratic. The two are not, in fact, contradictory, for the nature and quality of educational theory leads easily to stereotyping ('lower-class children are verbally deprived'), while the 'conventional wisdom' of the teaching profession leads to individualizing ('all children are different'), accentuated by the problems of privacy, immediacy, and autonomy already discussed. These three characteristics of the teacher's everyday world in turn accentuate the importance of generating a shared perspective with some, or all, of one's colleagues, to mitigate the isolation. Given the unique nature of each classroom encounter, the need for shared perspectives for added strength and to develop 'fellow feeling' accentuates stereotyping.

Shibutani (1955) argued that perspectives are essential if people are to 'conceive of their changing world as relatively stable, orderly and predictable'. Given the immediacy of classroom events, teachers need to view pupils as stable and predictable. Their perspectives on pupils, as well as being a confusing mixture of stereotype and idiosyncrasy, operate at several different levels.

Perspectives in the school

The most generalized level of perspective concerns the intake of the school and is shared by all staff. Then come perspectives held by all teachers about sub-groups of pupils, such as 'C-streamers', 'blacks', or 'lower-class' children. These are followed by perspectives shared by sub-groups of staff – either about the pupils as a whole, or about specific pupils they teach. In the former case the sub-group of staff form a reference group for each other, while in the second they may have little in common but their contact with the pupils concerned. The next level concerns the staffroom labelling of particular pupils. Conversation between teachers about individual pupils solidifies the individual perceptions into a reputation, which travels before the pupil into new classroom encounters. Lacey (1970, p. 179) describes how disconcerting it is for a master when a pupil reputation is disturbed. The dangers of acquiring a bad reputation are apparent to pupils. One girl at St Luke's told me how, one lunchtime, a teacher prevented her giving her unwanted portion of cottage pie to her friend Lorraine. Katherine commented:

> I felt like saying 'Would you rather it went to the pigs?' but you can't rebel against one teacher because if you do *all* the teachers are against you because you're rebellious!

A clearer account of labelling theory would be hard to find!

Lastly we have the perceptions of individual teachers about specific pupils they teach. In primary schools, where each teacher spends most of her time with one class and they see only her, her perspectives may be crucial for the pupil's school career. Here the concept of the 'self-fulfilling prophecy' becomes operative, as I argue below. At secondary level, where pupils see ten or more teachers, it is possible for a pupil to be seen very differently by various staff, if they have not acquired a definitive label. Many do acquire reputations, and these too will be self-fulfilling.

The self-fulfilling prophecy

The idea of the self-fulfilling prophecy came originally from Merton, but its educational implications were made famous – or rather infamous – by Rosenthal and Jacobson (1968). The basic assumption is simple: that if teachers believe a child to be stupid they will treat it differently, the child will internalize that judgement and behave accordingly, and a vicious circle is set up.

Rosenthal and Jacobson were the first researchers to try and demonstrate the existence of self-fulfilling prophecies in schools, and they started an acrimonious debate. Subsequently, however, other researchers have demonstrated teacher expectancies coming true in properly designed studies (reviewed by Brophy and Good, 1974). In the rest of this chapter I am going to accept that teacher labels do exert influence on pupils, and concentrate on how they are acquired.

Many pupils are labelled by their placement in particular groups within the organization. Allocation to the 'C' stream rather than the 'A' stream is the most obvious example, but staff will have expectations about other groups: forms, years, houses, and so forth. However, at classroom level, individual reputations are more important, although we only understand the general guidelines along which they are formed. Teachers certainly pick up 'clues' from what, following Goffman (1971) we will call the pupil's 'personal front'. In Chapter 2, I used the idea of a stage set in the discussion of physical context. Goffman goes on to relate the physical setting to his notion of 'personal front' as follows:

> If we take the term 'setting' to refer to the scenic parts of expressive equipment, one may take the term 'personal front' to refer to the other items of expressive equipment, the items that we must intimately identify with the performer himself and that we naturally expect will follow the performer wherever he goes. As part of the personal front we may include: insignia of office or rank; clothing; sex; age; and racial characteristics; size and looks; posture; speech patterns; facial expressions; bodily gestures; and the like. (p. 24)

Many of these characteristics are used constantly by teachers in building up and reinforcing stereotypes. Race is crucial. Teachers in the USA have low expectations of Mexican, negro, and Puerto Rican pupils, while in Britain negative stereotypes are held about West Indians and Asians. Once the teacher has a low estimate of a pupil's abilities she does not attempt to teach as much material or expect responses of the same quality. Then, teachers have different standards for the two sexes (Brophy and Good, 1974). At the junior school level teachers underestimate the abilities of boys, especially boys from working-class homes, and reprimand them more often. Somewhere during adolescence the bias swings the other way, and girls are no longer expected to be academically successful. The work of David Hartley (1978) shows differential teacher beliefs about young children in Britain; as Guttentag and Bray (1976) do for the USA. Katherine Clarricoates (1980) has carried out participant observation in four primary schools in England, where teacher perceptions of sex differences were modified by the social class nature of the intake. Clarricoates found teacher perceptions of sex differences led to different classroom behaviour. For example:

> Craig and Edward were involved in a game of plasticine and both are seized with a fit of laughter. They are allowed to carry on. But . . . (when) two girls were caught up in a similar game and became noisy the teacher classed it as 'giggling hysterically' and told the girls to 'calm down'. (p. 31)

The complex issue of the role of the school in sex role socialization is discussed in Delamont (1980).

The available evidence on how teachers form their assessments suggests that the characterizations of a pupil's home background are more likely to be based on the personal front displayed than on any systematic evidence or theoretical postulate. Scruffy, dirty, 'unsuitably' dressed pupils will be seen as coming from 'poor' homes. Poor homes mean low IQ, lots of siblings, lack of parental involvement, poor language skills, and behaviour problems, so the teacher *knows* she is in for trouble! The use of such clues by teachers, and their long-term consequences, can be seen for the USA in Rist's (1970) work in a negro kindergarten, and for Britain in Sharp and Green (1975) and King (1978). In both studies teachers use a mixture of 'theory' and 'practice' to interpret the clues, and place pupils into stereotyped categories on the basis of the interpretation.

Guilty knowledge

The pupils' personal fronts are not the only source of information for teachers. Society gives teachers the right of access to what we can call 'guilty knowledge' about pupils. School staff are allowed, or expected, to have access to information about pupils which is not publicly available: IQ scores or reading ages, other teachers' opinions and marks, confidential medical and family data, and so forth. Such materials can be very private – such as a child's father being in prison – or relatively trivial – such as a boy's middle name being Lancelot or Marmaduke. Names are a very good example of what is meant by guilty knowledge. Even in the formal boys' school where surnames are used, masters have access to boys' first names. Only in the more 'progressive' schools (e.g. Swidler, 1979) will pupils have legitimate access to staff first names.

I am not trying to argue that staff should not have this private information – it may be in everyone's interest for them to do so. But the teacher's classroom behaviour may be considerably altered by its possession. During my fieldwork at St Luke's I noticed two girls 'getting away with' behaviour in the classroom which was reprimanded when others engaged in it. I discovered that staff meetings had discussed both girls, and decided to 'go easy' on them. One girl had a young stepmother who was having her first baby, the other's parents were involved in a stormy divorce. The staff decided that both girls were likely to be upset by their family situations, and therefore behaviour problems would be due to this disturbance and should be treated sympathetically.

Sizing-up pupils is a continuous process. The teacher is constantly observing pupils, reacting to them, observing their reactions, and so on. The teacher's actions are, in part, decided by what she sees – or rather her understanding of what she sees – but she also acts according to her perspective on her job. If she believes a child is not 'ready' to read she is unlikely to spend time trying to teach him to do so. Thus the classroom researcher must try to understand how the teacher perceives her job, for as Smith and Geoffrey put it: 'Teaching must be seen as an intellectual, cognitive activity. What goes on in the head of the teacher is a critical antecedent of what he does' (p. 96).

One interesting part of the systematic observation studies of pupils' engaged academic time has been a growing interest in the 'matching' of child and task. Bennett and Desforges (1984) found that tasks may be 'inappropriate' for the pupil for 50 per cent of class time: being either too hard or too easy. Obviously the teacher's assessment of the child and his or her abilities is an important part of her decision about what work to assign, so expectations set too low may be a cause of educational failure. Kathleen Wilcox's (1982) research in two contrasting elementary schools supports this view.

Segmentation and perspectives

While all teachers have perspectives on their job, the segmented nature of the profession means that the different sections have very different aims and outlooks on their task. Musgrove and Taylor (1969) showed differences between grammar, junior and secondary modern school staff regarding their role. Grammar school staff had a much more limited conception of their job, concentrated on moral and intellectual growth. They were not concerned with 'social' issues: education for citizenship, marriage or work. Secondary modern staff saw themselves involved with all aspects of their pupils' development. Among junior school teachers, those in middle-class neighbourhoods were closer to the grammar school staff, while those in working-class areas were closer to the secondary modern teachers. Infant teachers opted for a diffuse 'mothering' role, as Ronald King (1978) found a decade later.

Thus while *all* teachers stressed intellectual skills and moral training, those concerned with lower ability, very young, and/or working-class pupils saw themselves 'gentling the masses'. These differences are obviously related to the cleavages in the profession already discussed. Dodd (1974) showed ex-grammar school teachers working in comprehensive schools were changing their role concept towards that of the secondary modern teachers studied by Musgrove and Taylor. The only large-scale, systematic study of British teachers' aims was undertaken by Ashton and her collaborators (1975). In a national survey of 1513 primary teachers they found both a great deal of consensus and two distinct sub-groups: traditionalists and progressives. Overall the teachers gave high priority to basic skills (reading, literacy, oracy and numeracy), and to the children being brought up as acceptable and accepting members of their community. They rejected, or thought unimportant, aesthetics, science, a second language, sex education and religion, especially comparative religion. Ashton shows a large number of teachers believing that their work should be concentrated on conventional primary school aims: basic skills and social adjustment. Ashton's (1981) restudy in 1977 showed little change in attitudes among primary teachers.

The language of perspectives

One interesting point about Ashton's work is the simple language in which the aims were presented. For example, the child should be able to: 'write legibly and know how to present his work attractively', 'listen with concentration and understand', and 'have a wide vocabulary'. None are expressed in the technical terminology of Piaget, Bruner, Bernstein or other theorists. This may seem insulting to the teachers, but an acquaintance with teachers' speech soon shows that the everyday language is an accurate reflection of their usage. Ashton's own study makes the point neatly. At an early phase of the project 54 teachers produced their own statements of their aims. They averaged only four statements. These were very wide in scope, at a high level of generality, and 73 per cent fell into three basic categories (one moral, one all-round development, and one intellectual). Most were open-ended and could not be operationalized in the classroom, or evaluated. In subsequent discussion groups it became clear that the majority of statements (72 per cent) were based on personal opinion only, while only a tiny fraction (4 per cent) were drawn from academic sources or experience. This disregard of research evidence is not surprising when one remembers the findings of Cane and Schroeder (1970). They found that more than half the teachers they sampled were completely unfamiliar with the research of eleven out of fourteen prominent authors. Well over three-quarters never saw any of the educational research journals.

Jackson (1968) has made very similar observations about American teachers: 'One of the most notable features of teacher talk is the absence of a technical vocabulary' (p. 148). He points out that it is characterized by 'conceptual simplicity' and a simplistic attitude to causality. He summarized the teacher's world as follows: 'Lacking a technical vocabulary, skimming the intellectual surface of the problems they encounter, fenced in, as it were, by the walls of their concrete experience . . .' (p. 148). It is rather frightening to imagine such people in charge of intellectual growth in others! However, as Jackson goes on to argue such qualities may be essential for survival in the face of the immediacy, privacy and autonomy of the classroom. Teachers have to *ad-lib*, and ad-libbing is an essential element in good teaching. Good teachers report that they find it more fruitful to follow the natural rhythm of classroom events rather than hold to preconceived plans.

Ann and Harold Berlak (1981, pp. 235–6) are sharply critical of this view of teachers' intellectual rigour. They state:

> We are especially wary of 'scientific' attributions of irrationality levelled at low-status groups . . . the traits these researchers attribute to teachers resemble those attributed to low-status, historically-oppressed groups . . . racial or ethnic minorities, working-class poor. We should recall in this regard that the largest numbers of teachers . . . are women.

The Berlaks argue that classroom teachers may be more expert about schools than so-called 'experts', and be operating with a much more subtle, reflexive, conceptual schema than researchers have tapped.

Researchers certainly differ in the complexity and subtlety of the teacher perspectives they manage to elicit. The typifications of pupils elicited by Nell Keddie (1971), Hargreaves *et al.* (1975) and Peter Woods (1979) reveal this variation. What we still lack is detailed research on the relations between teacher beliefs and practices.

Reconciling the irreconcilable

Work on teachers' aims tells us nothing about what they actually *do*. Many of the aims in the Ashton study are difficult to implement, and some may be contradictory. The two rated most important are happiness and reading, yet we can all imagine a pupil whose (short-term?) happiness is jeopardized by a teacher's insistence that he reads. Teachers are balancing contradictory aims all the time, but we know little about how they go about it, or how they view the necessity. This is odd when many have argued that the teacher's role is so diffuse because it involves the constant reconciliation of the unreconcilable.

Discrepancies will occur at many levels. Teachers have to reconcile different aspects of their careers in the profession, their position in the school, and their objectives inside the classroom. Every teacher has to decide whether to change schools, ask for more examination classes, push 3C to finish Napoleon this lesson or have a discussion, or to tell June off for being out of her seat. Teaching is a continuous process of decision-making, and the pupils are never static. Rather they are a seething mass forcing the teacher to make new decisions constantly. There is little research on teachers' perspectives on their day-to-day work at any of these levels. On career planning we have Becker (1952), Peterson (1964) and Grace (1972 and 1978), and at classroom level Smith and Geoffrey (1968), Adelman (1975), Woods (1980), and Ann and Harold Berlak (1981).

Classroom perspectives

This book is concerned with classrooms and the perspectives teachers have on their work therein. These classroom perspectives have two main foci: control and instruction. Without control, the teacher cannot instruct, and instruction is her *raison d'être*.

Control and instruction

The pupils must learn what they can, and cannot, do and what academic work is expected. The teacher, therefore, must decide what her expectations and limits of tolerance are, define them to the class, and get her definitions accepted. Concern with fixing the limits, and getting them accepted, preoccupies the teacher. This concern is the main source of tension in the teaching relationship, a tension well captured by Lacey (1970):

71

> Educationalists and even sociologists frequently use gardening analogies . . . about . . . education, e.g. 'cultivating' pupils. The metaphor is totally misleading. I have yet to hear of a gardener being reduced to a nervous wreck by errant plants. (p. 170)

Teachers vary widely in their definitions of acceptable behaviour, as all pupils become aware, and in their ability to impose their definition of order upon the pupils. The variety of standards imposed upon pupils can be seen vividly in the twelve types of classroom regime demonstrated by Bennett and Jordan (1975), and is caught qualitatively in Gibson's (1973) interviews with teachers. Gibson quotes many teachers who show preoccupation with decisions about disciplinary standards and their imposition. For example:

> It's a case of just making it clear that in your lessons they behave in such and such a way. (p. 89)
>
> I draw the imaginary line – they may come up to that line and they put their toe on it – but God help them if they put their toe over it. (p. 159)
>
> Get them to realize that if they do what you want, then you will be quite fair with them. (p. 58)
>
> It is noise of the wrong kind which disturbs and creates tension. (p. 8)
>
> I don't tolerate this business of walking about. (p. 67)
>
> I will have attention. I won't teach without it. (p. 162)
>
> I find that children like to be controlled, because then they know where they are. (p. 75)
>
> It appears that you must constantly get on to the children – in the sense that you deflate them; you've got to make them toe the line all the time, you cannot assume that they'll come in, and sit down and get on with the job. (p. 188)

The teacher's desire to maintain control comes from at least three sources. Firstly, the staff of a particular school have common standards about control which the individual teacher breaks at her peril. Her colleagues are the reference group for her control standards. This is well captured by Martyn Denscombe (1980) who found that the secondary teachers he studied saw noise as the symbol of control. Noise from other teachers' rooms was a signal of a breakdown of control, noise from their own an admission of loss of control. He says:

> It was noise created by pupils, rather than by music or audio-visual aids, which constituted significant clues because . . . it could be taken to be indicative of a lack of control in the classroom.

A similar point is made for American junior schools by McPherson (1972) where competent teachers kept their doors open. Ronald King (1978, p. 73) found an infant school head using this criterion: 'Miss Brown at Burnley Road . . . liked the classroom doors left open. Having the door open was the sign of a "Good teacher" . . .' With an open door the 'busy hum' of the controlled classroom could be heard, and judged. Bullivant (1978) also points out that pupils can judge teachers according to the amount of noise emanating from their classes.

Each teacher will have her own ideas about the amount of control she can maintain and how much she needs to teach successfully. Finally she will be aware of the degree of control the pupils expect and want her to exercise. Sometimes these three standards will not coincide, and then the teacher must reconcile them as best she can.

Lacey gives a neat example of a maths master 'blowing his top', and relates the incident to the master's worries about the group's academic progress: 'We've not done a tenth of the syllabus' (1970, p. 179). The teacher is always concerned with the academic progress of the class. She must decide what to teach them next period, next week, next term, next year. Also she must decide what level of work she wants from them, and how to communicate the standard and enforce it. In the academic secondary school she will worry about progress through a syllabus, in the primary school about individual progress in basic skills, but the dilemma is similar. Gibson's interviewees, drawn from all types of school, exemplify this:

> I don't want to go into class and clean the board for inspiration. I want to know beforehand what I'm going to do. (p. 90)

In the grammar school we are orientated to GCE and A Level . . . the whole class has to do it. (p. 70)

We do the Beta arithmetic, and mine should be on book 11, though the backward ones are on book 1. We don't laboriously go through each, page by page. (p. 100)

I was alarmed at the end of my first year . . . that I had been giving kids . . . work that was either too easy . . . or too hard for them . . . this year I've been quicker to see what children are capable of doing . . . (p. 40)

I'm worried about whether I'm going too fast for the slow ones . . . I probably go miles above their heads. (1973, p. 4)

Becker (1952) long ago showed similar concerns exercising Chicago public school teachers, who contrasted the different styles of work in good and bad schools:

At S—, if you had demonstrations in chemistry they had to be pretty flashy, lots of noise and smoke, before they'd get interested in it. That wasn't necessary at L—. Now in a school like the D— you're just not expected to complete all that work. It's almost impossible. For instance, in the second grade we're supposed to cover nine spelling words in a week. Well I can do that up here . . . but the best class I ever had at the D— was only able to achieve six. . . . So I never finished the year's work in spelling. I couldn't. And I really wasn't expected to.

The Berlaks (1981) have focused their research effort on the dilemmas which face all teachers, suggesting that these are equally acute in the control, curriculum and social areas of classroom life.

Conclusion

This, then, is the teacher. The occupant of a diffuse role, facing a large number of pupils who have to be controlled and, ideally, taught. Her working situation is characterized by the peculiar features of privacy, immediacy and autonomy, all of which are double-edged: strengthening and weakening her position in negotiations. Her greatest resource, knowledge, is also her

74

Achilles' heel. She should share perspectives with, and draw support from her colleagues in the school – who may offer practical help to mitigate certain problems. Her main preoccupation is to size up the pupils she faces and to decide what to do with them – a task in which she is not aided by research evidence or grand theory. The next chapter looks at the subject of her concern – the pupils.

4 The protagonists: the pupils

Imagine that you are a distinguished educator, visiting an American teachers' college to give a lecture. You go into an ordinary classroom and find the students waiting for you. At 2.00 you begin, and all seems normal. Most of your audience seem vaguely involved, and you congratulate yourself on another well-earned fee. 2.15 strikes. Suddenly the audience are agog. On the edges of their chairs, they are nodding and smiling, writing everything down. 'Great', you think, 'Now I've really got them interested' . . . 2.30 strikes. 'Help!' Equally suddenly, the audience has fallen apart. Everyone is yawning and whispering. No one writes. Half of them are staring out of the window. 'Christ', you think, 'what on earth have I said? No standards left in these colleges' . . . 2.45 and life is back to normal – this is where you came in . . .

That lecture sounds like every teacher's nightmare. In fact, the audience were behaving according to a pre-arranged plan, to help a psychologist called Susan Klein (1971) show that student behaviour can alter teaching style. Somewhere at the back of the room an observer was coding your teaching. When the audience was super-attentive your teaching was much warmer towards them; when they were behaving badly, you became critical. In short, the students were manipulating you.

There are of course enormous problems, both practical and moral, about repeating this experiment at school level. In addition, it is much too contrived to fit happily into the interactionist framework of this book. However, I want to show that existing research done at school level can be used to produce conclusions supporting Klein from an interactionist perspective. Part of Klein's success derived from the whole student audience being involved. One student staring out of the window is a deviant: a whole class staring out of the window is a demonstration of pupil power unnerving to the most experienced teacher! Pupil power is therefore group power. A pupil's strength is directly related to the number of classmates who can be mobilized in support – who share the same definition of the situation.

The pupils' role

This chapter is a distorted mirror image of Chapter 3. It deals with ideas of roles, personal front and reputation – but it differs sharply over the idea of power. Whereas the teacher's role is one of socially accepted – legitimate – dominance, the pupil's role is one of subserviance. Any power pupils exercise is not socially sanctioned but illegitimate. Pupils are expected to learn, and to behave in ways that will facilitate learning, whether this is by sitting quietly absorbing the teacher's lectures, or busying themselves with worksheets, apparatus and 'resources'. They are expected to let their speech, dress, morals and behaviour be monitored and corrected, and their state of knowledge constantly examined and criticized.

However, not all pupils accept the constraints of the role, and it would be dangerous to take teacher dominance for granted, as many researchers have done. Although it is the norm, it may not always be in operation, and the classroom researcher must be sensitive to violations and counter examples. Traditional classroom research of the type popularized by Flanders (1970) assumes that the teacher is the dominant influence on classroom interaction. These researchers believe that an indirect teacher produces a democratic classroom climate, and a directive one an authoritarian regime. However, the empirical basis for this belief is non-existent. It is taken for granted. In fact, Klein has demonstrated very neatly that the reverse may be the case.

Pupil power and friendship

The pupils' power is directly related to the numbers they can mobilize against the teacher. To have power, the pupil needs help from her friends. Pupil friendship groups, unlike those of teachers, have received a great deal of research attention. The conventional wisdom on the subject is expressed in the following quotation from Morrison and McIntyre (1973):

> Whether or not a class has any formal social organization, it has an informal social structure which, with pupils over the age of about seven, and when the class has been together for some time, tends to be relatively stable. Sub-groups of various sizes are formed, either integrated within a cohesive class group, or indifferent or hostile to other sub-groups . . . Membership of such informal groups is voluntary, and that members continue to belong to them is due to a shared acceptance of, and preference for, certain ways of behaving. (p. 134)

The well known British studies of pupil friendship groups: Hargreaves (1967), Lacey (1970) and Willis (1977), are all about boys in state secondary schools. Data on girls, pupils in private schools, and younger children are rarer. Hargreaves, Lacey and Willis all researched streamed boys' schools and showed how academic segregation leads to polarized sub-cultures within the school. In the upper streams boys looked to a pro-school clique of 'goodies', and in the lower to an anti-school group of 'baddies'.

Fascinating as such studies are, they reveal little about classroom behaviour. We can all imagine that, as John Furlong (1976) puts it: 'even the most delinquent pupils will be well-behaved in certain circumstances'. Similarly, we all know that good pupils sometimes create trouble for their staff. Nothing in conventional peer group research will predict, or even explain, these deviations. When studying classroom interaction we need a less static concept than the clique – a concept that helps us understand how pupils sometimes act together to impose their definition of the situation upon the teacher, and at other times leave a trouble-maker isolated, and thus vulnerable to teacher authority. Furlong offers us a more dynamic notion with the 'interaction set'. He argues that 'classroom situations change in the meaning they have for pupils, and as they change, so will the pupils' assessments of how to behave'. Furlong therefore defines an interaction set as a group which 'at any one time will be those pupils who perceive what is happening in a similar way, communicate with each other, and define appropriate action together'. The concept can best be demonstrated from the following three incidents drawn from Furlong's fieldwork on girls in an inner-city school with a majority of black pupils. In the first incident Carol and Diane fail to mobilize an interaction set to support them in an act of defiance; in the second they succeed tacitly with a small group; while in the third they form part of a large interaction set outlawing one deviant:

1. (Carol and Diane) are late for the lesson, and are talking to each other in the corridor. Angela tries to distinguish herself from them in the teacher's eyes by 'telling on them'. When Mrs Alan comes in, Carol and Diane are missing, she asks where they are. Angela says they were in the last lesson.
Angela: 'Them lot are outside, Miss.'
Mrs Alan goes out and sends in Carol and Diane, who enter laughing loudly and start to sit down. They are followed in by Mrs Alan, who shouts 'Stand at the front'. They continue to laugh and look round the room, though less confidently than before. Other class members are no longer laughing with them, and Carol and Diane's eyes rove the room, but come into contact with no one in particular.

2. Eight of the girls are sitting round the same bench in the science lab. Carol and Diane run in thirty minutes late and sit down with them all.

Carol (to the whole table): 'I went home to get some tangerines.'
Mrs Newman: 'Where have you been?'
Diane (aggressively): 'Dentist . . .'
Mrs Newman: 'Where have you been?'
Carol (aggressively): 'None of your business.'
Mrs Newman ignores, or does not hear this remark.
The interaction set is much larger . . . ten girls are involved.

3. Debbie is eating an ice lolly. Mrs Alan tells her to put it in the bin, but Debbie refuses and turns round in her seat to face the rest of the class . . . when she continues to refuse . . . Mrs Alan (says) 'Right, you are in school to do as you are told. When you have put your sweet in the bin as I asked you you can have your hat back.'
Debbie: 'You give me that hat back. I paid for it. Give it back to me!'
As she says this she looks towards Diane and Carol but they continue with their work. Debbie sulks for the rest of the lesson, making no attempt to do any work whatsoever. She is totally ignored by the rest of the class, who carry on working enthusiastically.

Here we see how pupils offer each other support by eye contact, laughter, and sympathetic silence, and withdraw it by avoiding eye contact, unsympathetic silence, and 'telling on' each other.

Some commentators have suggested that John Furlong is actually describing a sex or race difference, because his data are about British West Indian girls, rather than offering a critique of Hargreaves's and Lacey's work on white males. Until we have more studies of pupils of both sexes, various ethnic groups inside classrooms and around the school, this argument cannot be resolved. Mary Fuller (1980) has also studied British West Indian girls in a London school, and agrees with Furlong that a fluid notion like 'interaction set' best characterizes the variety of their classroom behaviour. Fuller's sample was different from either Furlong's or those of Willis, Hargreaves and Lacey in one way, however. Her girls were hardworking and ambitious (they wanted qualifications and 'good' jobs) but were also badly behaved in school. Fuller writes:

Unlike other pupils who were similarly pro-education, the black girls were not pro-school . . . Their intolerance of the daily routines and their criticisms of much that went on inside school were marked . . . Despite their critical view of school the black girls did not define it as 'irrelevent'.

Fuller says that most aspiring pupils in the school not only did their work, but also looked attentive in class, arrived punctually and offered staff a certain 'respect'. In contrast:

The black girls conformed to the stereotypes of the good pupil only in so far as they worked conscientiously . . . But they gave all the appearances in class of not doing so . . .

Fuller suggests her sample's behaviour is parallel to that reported by Werthman (1963) in the USA for negro males. She feels that the superficially 'bad' behaviour in class enabled the girls to mask their academic and job aspirations from the black males who would have rejected and ridiculed them.

Overall it seems more sensible to keep both the concept of the peer group and that of the interaction set as working hypotheses when examining pupils' school lives. We also need to explain why certain interaction sets coalesce and others do not, or why some pupils are more successful than others in mobilizing them. The answer to the former lies in pupil definitions of the situation; to the latter in various individuals' power and status in the peer group and the classroom. Pupil perspectives on the classroom form the second half of this chapter, following a discussion of pupils' statuses with peers and teachers.

Pupil status in school and classroom

The pupil's status in the classroom has two aspects: status with peers and with teachers. While it is true that in all schools the pupil who is too popular with the staff may be disliked by all the other pupils – the 'teacher's pet' syndrome – in general we can contrast situations in which status vis-à-vis teachers and peer group coincide with those in which they are diametrically opposed. In classrooms where the predominant perspective is anti-authority, anti-teacher, anti-school, high status in the peer group will guarantee unpopularity with the staff. In the hard-working top stream the reverse will be the case, and the successful scholar and captain of football are likely to have friends and be well thought of by the staff. In classes which have mixed batches of pupils – by race, sex, abilities and dispositions – complex variations in pupil-pupil and pupil-teacher relationship will be found, as in Fuller's (1980) research.

Reading Hargreaves's (1967) study of Lumley secondary modern, we can all imagine that the high status trouble-makers of 4C and 4D would have less difficulty in defining a situation as worthy of disruption than low prestige boys, and would be more able to mobilize an interaction set. Thus, while accepting Furlong's strictures that the conventional concept of a peer group is too static to capture the complexities of classroom interaction, I would still argue that cliques do exist and status in them is important. In the more menacing situation described by Werthman (1963), peer group power among the delinquent gangs is directly related to physical strength and the fear it creates in teachers. Writing about male negro delinquents in California, Werthman describes how certain students have power over their staff. 'The sources of this power stem from the possibilities of physical assault on teachers and an ability to keep the class in constant turmoil.' As one boy put it, 'When you get a good grade, sometimes you know the teacher is afraid of you.' In both these schools physical prowess gives a boy status among his peers, and this leads to power in mobilizing interaction sets. Skill at disrupting lessons is also relevant, and here a pupil's reputation as a trouble-maker will be central. Paul Willis's (1977) study of 'lads' and 'ear'oles' in a Midlands secondary school reveals the same brutish anti-school culture. His 'lads' apparently had no difficulty in mobilizing disruptive interaction sets.

Apart from physical strength among certain male sub-cultures, deep involvement in 'youth culture' will give high status in some peer groups. Knowledge about pop music, skilful dancing, fashionable clothes and successful relationships with the opposite sex can all help a pupil towards popularity. Lacey

(1970) writes of a boy, Russell, who set out to cultivate a more fashionable image, and became a disc jockey at a local club where he met girls, in order to improve his status inside Hightown Grammar. As interest in such matters percolated the top stream, Russell's status improved and he ended his career at Hightown successful with his peers and his work. In the 1960s, researchers argued that involvement in 'youth culture' went hand in hand with an anti-school attitude and rejection of intellectual and cultural values. Since then the nature of youth culture has changed and its relationship to school is much more complicated, so that involvement with pop culture no longer implies an anti-school stance (Murdock and Phelps, 1973). Fans of some pop are pro-school, fans of another type are hostile. Adolescent sub-culture takes a variety of forms today which can be found co-existing within the same school. Larkin (1979) states that inside one suburban school in the USA (Utopia High) there were six distinct sub-cultures: all varieties of 'youth culture'. He identified three different 'leading crowds' (that is loosely pro-school groups): the 'intellectuals', the 'politicos' and the 'jock/rah-rahs'.

The 'jock/rah-rah' crowd is the conventional high school student culture of male athletes and girl cheerleaders, familiar both from the work of Coleman (1961) and from *Grease* and *Happy Days*. This group is the source of 'school spirit', and its members are having a good time but are also college-bound (i.e. high achievers). In Utopia High, this group were upper middle-class Protestants in origin. Opposed to the jock/rah-rah group was a mainly Jewish, highly academic, but left-wing group – the 'politicos' – who campaigned for student power in the school. The third pro-school group was also heavily Jewish in origin, and was, Larkin (1979, p. 72) claims, 'rare'. Indeed he says:

> Nowhere in the sociological literature has such a group been found in high schools. At Utopia High, I found students who were reading Thomas Mann, T. S. Eliot, and Karl Marx for their own edification. . . . One student was planning to live in Paris after graduation to study the flute . . .

Larkin's surprise at discovering such a peer group might be

mitigated if he were to read Bullivant's (1978) study of a school where half the boys belonged to just such a culture. One group of girls at St Luke's, who called themselves 'the intellectuals' (and who were labelled by classmates 'swots and weeds') had a younger version of this academic orientation (Delamont, 1976b).

Larkin found three anti-school groups at Utopia High: hippies (smoking pot and yearning for the 1960s), greasers (yearning for the 1950s, white, working-class and identifying with Fonz in *Happy Days*) and the negros, who suffered *de facto* segregation in the bottom tracks (streams) of the school. There were also pupils who were not identified with any of these student subcultures. Larkin's book is not primarily about classroom behaviour, but it is clear that a white or Jewish girl in the intellectual group, preparing for entry to an elite college is not going to smoke dope in lessons, as the hippies regularly did. Student cultures at Utopia High may seem remote from the British comprehensives studied by Meyenn (1980), Woods (1979) and Ball (1981). Yet one problem Larkin faced, making the 'good' pupils come alive for the reader, is shared by most school ethnographers.

Bad pupils, and those becoming go-go dancers to gain status, are entertaining to write about. The conflict between peer status and unpopularity with staff has a dramatic element which makes it vivid to the reader. Hargreaves (1967) and Lacey (1970) portray boys who are popular with staff and peers, but their portraits are less colourful than those of rebels. Hargreaves describes the head boy, Adrian, who is top of his class and captain of football, yet is the most popular boy in his form. Lacey presents a case study of Adam, a pro-school conformist, and writes:

> (In class) he was alert, clean and well dressed. He seemed to radiate well-being and self-confidence . . . At school he was popular with staff and never lacked a large number of friends among the pupils . . . At home his parents were immensely proud of his success and never stinted their support. (pp. 127–8)

84

At St Luke's there was a girl, Jackie, who was similarly blessed. Academically successful, good at games, musical, and pretty, she was popular with her classmates and well regarded in the staffroom. The teachers valued her efficiency, tidiness, pleasant manners and good work. The nearest thing to a criticism I ever heard was the maths mistress's comment, 'she only answers if she's sure she's right'.

It is very difficult to write vividly about such paragons of virtue and make them come up off the page for the reader. Jackie sounds like a prig though she was a friendly, intelligent girl who deserved her popularity. Adam and Adrian probably deserved theirs but they too sound wooden. Conflict between pupils and school is easier to dramatize. Researchers have a tendency to concentrate on the deviant, colourful or bizarre pupil, and can fall into the trap of glorifying the kind of pupil in their research reports they would find unpleasant to teach, employ or introduce to their parents. Willis (1977), for example, wants the reader to rejoice in the anti-school attitudes of 'the lads' and share their derision of the 'ear'oles'. It is very important that researchers studying schools do not fall into this trap of over-identification with one subculture so it blinds them to other perspectives on the interaction. McRobbie and Garber (1975) have demonstrated how many male researchers have adopted the world view of their male informants and lost their proper detachment about other participants in their informants' social setting. Pupils have strong views, but researchers have to be careful not to be seduced by them. Peter Woods (1979, p. 64) found some girls who disliked a classmate they saw as a swot:

> Karen: If we do anything wrong, we get shouted at. If Jane does it, it's 'Jane, do stop, please, dear' . . .
> Lisa: She *always* does homework, so never gets into trouble . . .
> Karen: One teacher said, 'This is a girl who's going to get on in life'. It makes you sick.
> Lisa: Reading a passage in French, she'd volunteer. Beefy would say 'I think you've done enough, Jane.' She'd say, 'I want to do it, I want to.'

Here we see a pupil the teachers probably like who is unpopular with classmates. Her classmates' opinions are relevant to their status in school, but the researcher has to be careful to collect Jane's views too, and remember that she too has a legitimate perspective on schooling.

Pupils like Jane, Jackie at St Luke's, Adam and Adrian share staff perspectives about what school is for and what legitimate behaviour includes and excludes. Given their shared outlook, their likes and dislikes are going to coincide. If a pupil such as Jackie or Adam decides that a lesson is suitable for disruption their definition is likely to be acceptable to less compliant pupils. If a class bores or distresses the ideal pupil her classmates are likely to agree!

Pupil reputations

Status in the peer group, therefore, relates to classroom action. Allied to clique status is teacher expectation, discussed in Chapter 3 from the teacher's angle. Pupils know about the importance of their reputations, which are reified in the staff-room and travel before them into each new classroom encounter. There are at least three aspects to a pupil reputation recognized by their 'owners': ability, effort and behaviour.

The pupil believed by the teacher to be of high ability has a head start in the classroom. As Brophy and Good (1974) have shown, teachers give 'clever' students every advantage over their classmates during instruction. They wait longer for them to answer, offer more clues, rephrase their questions more helpfully, and accept a wider range of responses. They assume that the bright pupil will eventually reach the answer and behave accordingly. This is, of course, how the self-fulfilling prophecy works: teachers encourage the clever pupil to think and rethink. Such qualitative and quantitative differences in teacher-pupil interaction, based on the teacher's *beliefs* about pupil abilities, have been demonstrated in all types of school, most recently, by Galton and Delafield (1981). What is not clear, however, is whether pupils are aware of these variations and the cumulative effect of establishing a reputation for being good in class.

Ability and effort

The girls at St Luke's certainly accepted that popularity with staff was related to ability in their subjects, but they did not appear to have any detailed knowledge of differences in teacher-pupil interactions relating to ability. In their eyes the good pupil should:

> Try to be good at the subject.
> Always have the right answer.
> The better you are the better they are likely to like you, but I think it's basically liking the subject.
> It helps to be good at the subject.

In addition, several girls mentioned that a teacher could become fond of the pupil who could be relied on for correct answers. One girl told me: 'Miss Paris used to dote on Mandy before she left – Mandy always had the right answers if no one else did'. It was recognized that such a favoured pupil could 'get away with' things others could not, as the girls interviewed by Woods (1979) apparently recognized.

Not everyone can be clever. However, anyone can try hard, and the St Luke's girls saw effort as an equally important element in building good relationships with staff. Good pupils:

> Work hard and try hard – doing your best.
> Work well, try their hardest, answer a lot in class and pay attention. Teachers like people who just improve every term and try their best.
> All teachers like people who try, are hardworking.
> I think just to work hard.

Unpopular pupils, on the other hand:

> Can't be bothered.
> Not attending, not learning.
> Unwillingness to work – laziness.
> People that don't try.
> People who never put their hands up and even try to answer a question.

These pupil perceptions were 'correct' in that the St Luke's staffroom did value ability and effort. The dangers of acquiring a bad reputation were well-known to pupils, as shown in Chapter 3 by the quote from Katherine about rebelliousness.

It must be stressed that the girls at St Luke's did not *want* teacher approval, and the quotations given here were elicited by asking 'If you had a sister coming here who wanted to be popular with teachers, what would you advise her to do?' All the girls said firmly that such an ambition was an unworthy one, which no self-respecting pupil could have. So the strategies they described were hypothetical, not accounts of their own behaviour in class. However they did believe that antagonizing teachers was a foolhardy thing to do. Mary Fuller's (1980) sample of black English girls were quite different. The girls believed that 'good' pupils were 'boring' and 'immature', and that teacher approval was not necessary for eventual success, because:

> in so far as public examinations were marked by people who did not know the candidates personally, pupils could expect to pass exams on the quality of their work rather than on the quality of their relationship with the teachers who taught them.

Fuller says other pupils (males, Asian and white girls) did not share this view. Research on how boys and other groups of girls see this issue is needed.

Good and bad homes

It is an asset for a pupil to be seen as coming from a 'good home', but while pupils are often aware of this they can do little about it. Teachers differentiate between 'rough', 'respectable' and 'affluent' working-class homes by means of visible clues – speech, clothing, manners, and so forth, and a pupil can learn to dissemble, though only at the cost of leading a double life or abandoning her home values in favour of the school's. This was always an acute problem for working-class entrants to grammar school, like the girl quoted by Jackson and Marsden (1966): 'Fairly early on I decided what changes I was going to make in my accent, and I made them' (p. 114). Pupils at expensive public schools are likely to have rather different problems over the link between home and school. At St Luke's, which was full of academic, upper middle-class girls, the staff differentiated between pupils from intellectual homes and those whose parents were merely wealthy, and therefore uncultured. ('Her father made all his money in scrap metal . . .'). In all such schools the staff may see themselves not 'gentling the masses' but civilizing the *nouveaux riches*. I found one girl who admitted her first reaction to St Luke's had been to change her Fife accent for a 'posh' one, but otherwise the girls seemed unaware of the staff attitudes. Girls from intellectual homes were seen as better pupils because their families valued scholarship. The most noticeable example of favouritism I saw came in history. Henrietta discovered she had forgotten her book and was sent to fetch it. Mrs Flodden held up the lesson for ten minutes, only starting to give notes when Henrietta returned. This was a unique event. Girls often went to fetch forgotten items, but I never saw a teacher wait for them. In effect, Mrs Flodden demonstrated that history could not take place without Henrietta. Henrietta explained this 'special relationship' as follows:

> I think Mrs Flodden likes me very much – because she knows my mother very well. I read quite a lot of history . . . of course Mrs Flodden – well she and (the headmistress) they're on terms – they come to our bonfire party every year. You know what I mean. They're all historians and they knew each other at Oxford and Cambridge.

Henrietta's mother is a university lecturer in history, and the other pupils recognized the 'edge' this gave her with Mrs Flodden. Such pupils bring their own problems for the teacher – their own power to the classroom. They have their family perspective on knowledge and access to material outside the school. They threaten the teacher, though in a manner quite different from the uncultured. Imagine yourself teaching history to the son of your old history professor, or physics to the daughter of the Nobel prize winner. You are entangled in a complex explanation of a key point when up goes the dreaded hand: 'Daddy's disproved that, Sir – there's a paper in this week's *Nature* . . .', or 'Mummy says no one believes *that* theory any more . . .'. Dropping such bombshells may make a pupil as powerful in the classroom as a reputation for beating up teachers or a name as 'the best mathematician in the school'.

Sizing up teachers

Just as teachers spend a great deal of time sizing up pupils, so too pupils are constantly engaged in sizing up their staff. Understanding pupil perspectives on teaching is as important for comprehending classroom encounters as teachers' social constructions of their pupils. Understanding the way pupils define the situation is the only way one can make sense of their actions.

The main strength of the teacher's position is that, in general, pupils want her to teach and to keep them in order. That is, they want her to organize an environment in which she can impart information, state problems with clarity, and help them to reach agreed solutions (Musgrove and Taylor, 1969). This is true both of low-ability pupils, such as those in the maths class described in Chapter 1, who might not seem to value order or instruction, and of more intellectual pupils.

Furlong (1976) shows how the low-ability West Indian girls he studied prized teachers who succeeded in convincing them they were learning. Carol, the most disruptive girl, said of her history master:

> You can't talk in Mr Mark's lesson, you just have to work . . . so after a while you work, and you enjoy it because you're learning a lot . . . Mr Marks would talk to us as well. Not talk them big words, you know, talk words we understood. . . .

Furlong goes on to contrast successful and unsuccessful lessons, and it is clear that successful lessons are those in which the girls feel they have been organized into learning something. Similar judgements can be found in Torode's (1976) work in a low stream of a Scottish comprehensive, Gannaway's (1976) in London, and Werthman's (1963) on Californian delinquents. Gannaway introduces his section on teacher authority with the heading 'Will the real Mr Teacher please make us sit down?', a comment which summarizes his pupils' attitudes. He quotes one boy whose ideal teacher is '. . . one that won't let you get too stroppy . . . and stops the lesson getting boring . . . he doesn't let the class get all stroppy and do what they want.'

Similarly, Werthman concludes his analysis of teacher-delinquent relations with the comment 'When gang members are convinced . . . that a teacher is really interested in teaching them something, and that efforts to learn will be rewarded' they behave perfectly well in class. A bargain satisfactory to both sides has been struck.

The highly academic middle-class girls of St Luke's had a very similar outlook. They judged teachers first and foremost on their abilities as instructors:

> . . . she makes you learn very, very hard . . . she really gets
>   you to learn.
> They are both very good teachers . . . make things very clear.
> She's especially well organized . . . keeps you working all the
>   time . . . doesn't let you stop for a minute. . . .

Bad teachers were characterized as follows:

> She's not a good teacher . . . she can't get her subject across
>   . . . she knows it, but . . .
> I don't think she's any good – she doesn't give any notes, and
>   when she explains things she goes so fast that you can't
>   really follow . . .
> She knows her subject, but I don't think she can get it across –
>   well, she can't get it across to me.

Getting the subject across is more important than the quality of the content for many pupils, who know little about history but know when they feel successful at it. The quality of the knowledge imparted by Miss Jean Brodie was seriously deficient, but she was regarded as an effective teacher (Spark, 1961).

American adolescents studied by Mary Metz (1978, pp. 74–7) shared these perceptions, respecting those staff who were fair, competent, cheerful and structured the lessons in a negotiable way. A typical pupil comment was: 'Last year I had Mrs

Cosgrove. She didn't have to be strict because we respected her
. . .' Teachers should be fair, neither making pets nor picking
on individuals (Musgrove and Taylor, 1969). They should be
cheerful and not nasty (Woods, 1979). Also they should support
their colleagues in public – for, as one St Luke's girl told me of
an unpopular mistress: 'She talks about other teachers quite
freely, which no teacher – no teacher – should *ever* do'. Pupils
often express severe criticisms of teachers who violate the major
constituents of the teaching role. As Brown (1965) points out, all
roles allow some 'creative interpretation', and using this leeway
is one way of becoming a 'character'. Violating what pupils
regard as major norms, however, means the teacher forfeits the
respect due to the role.

The teacher's personal front

Apart from her success at creating a learning atmosphere, and
her adherence to her role specifications, pupils judge teachers by
clues picked up from their personal fronts. Clearly many of the
characteristics Goffman (1971) suggests as significant aspects of
the personal front are important in school: gowns and overalls,
physical appearance, clothing, age, sex, race, speech, and the
paralinguistic features of posture, gesture and the like. Some of
these things are very obvious in schools. If the academic staff
wear gowns, the woodwork and cookery staff may look naked
without them. If all the staff are women but the music master,
his role deserves study. Does he avoid the staffroom, or occupy a
special role in it? If the latter, does it carry over into his
teaching? Does Miss X have a hole in her tights, Miss Y stutter,
and Miss Z smell? Such intimate matters can have profound
consequences for the classroom. Back in 1923 the first headmis-
tress of St Luke's, who had founded the school in the nineteenth
century, had a clear appreciation of the important clues pupils
pick up from the teacher's appearance. She wrote:

> There is, I know, in some minds an inclination to regard as
> unimportant, carefulness in dress and carriage and in speech!
> There are teachers whose classrooms always have a general air

of untidiness. These things are all factions [sic] in the sum total of the impression which the teacher's personality makes upon the pupil and are more clearly perceived and estimated by the pupil than the genius, or scholarship, or the special enthusiasm which are sometimes brought forward as extenuating circumstances.

The researcher should not scorn to use the messages conveyed by the teacher's personal front when studying classrooms. The paralinguistic phenomena – posture, gesture, facial expression and so forth – are difficult to study, but deserve attention. Walker and Adelman (1975b) have demonstrated how much research mileage there is in analysing such features. Differences in teacher-pupil relationship are frequently highlighted by paralinguistic behaviour. The teacher who spends her lessons seated at her desk, with a silent queue waiting to see her, can be visibly distinguished from her colleague who moves from desk to desk, often kneeling on the floor or putting her arm around a child. We expect them to be on different terms with their pupils, to praise different kinds of conduct, and even to have very different aims.

Teacher's speech

Pupils quickly spot idiosyncracies in the teacher's speech and accent, and often make judgements about the teacher's personality or mental state because of them. I collected two sets of material on this point from St Luke's, one an individual reaction by a girl to her history teacher, the other a more general commentary on a geography mistress. Georgina informed me that 'Mrs Flodden hasn't got what I call a teacher's voice'. When I tried to find out what she meant I received the elaboration 'Not the accent – others keep you awake – while Mrs Flodden gets so excited herself you end up getting bored'. Another girl did tell me that Mrs Flodden 'excites herself and bores me', which presumably expressed a similar point. The geography mistress, Miss Dale, had a mannerism which everyone she taught linked to a psychological state:

I feel sorry for her, because I feel she's a lonely person – nervous, shy – the way she says 'there' all the time.

Got a habit – always says 'there'. She gets flustered.

Rather nervous when she's teaching us, I don't know why.

Clothing

Clothes are an important element in the teacher's personal front. This has always been so between female staff and girls, and, with the increasing fashion-consciousness of men, is now as important among males. In a school which enforces a uniform, all the pupils' clothes-sense will be focused on the staff, and their judgements may be harsh. As with speech, moral or psychological states may be inferred from clothing. While at St Luke's Lorna said of her Spanish mistress 'She wears the most outlandish things, like a red skirt and pink tights!', a comment which was intended to tell me all I needed to know about the woman. Similarly, Penny summed up her opinions of another teacher with 'She wore red stockings – well, it just goes to show!'

Race and age

Black teachers are still rare in British schools, but the racial tensions described in *To Sir with Love* (Braithwaite, 1959) will exist where they do teach. Then, many British pupils are black, and they will have different perceptions of white and black staff (Furlong, 1983; Fuller, 1980). For the average British pupil, the teacher's race is less salient than two characteristics which all teachers possess: age and marital status. Age, and the amount of teaching experience it implies, forms one major dimension along which staff are placed. The St Luke's girls argued that younger staff were nicer and more sympathetic, while older ones are more efficient and keep better order:

The younger ones are usually the nicest – they haven't had so much experience. They're not embittered.

Mrs French gives the impression of the ancient teacher. You couldn't say anything about her was modern.

Not like the older ones, you can waste as much time as you like.

She's quite efficient . . . and can keep order . . . in class. It's to do with being older, she's had more experience.

The people who've been teaching . . . you know, the old school of teaching . . . some of the new teachers – something about them is they make the lessons more interesting. Some of the students – they're very nice, and they know how to make a boring lesson into a bright interesting lesson.

Similarly, Gannaway's (1976) work on London comprehensive pupils shows them using age and experience as relevant dimensions to judge classroom performance:

If a teacher's not too remote . . . like we had this Miss L last year and she was sort of like an overgrown one of us – dressed like us and everything, and you could really sort of talk to her.

Note here the link between youth, dress and approachability.

Stigma and marital status

Alongside age is marital status. Of course, it is only accessible to pupils when the teacher is a woman who uses Mrs or Miss, and so much of the following relates more to girls' perspectives. However, Liam Hudson (1968) shows boys relating classroom style to marital happiness. The unsympathetic, brusque, master ('Damm, there's those little wretches in 3B to take first. Will these little morons never learn Archimedes?') is perceived as unmarried or unhappily married ('How nice my single bed. How can people sleep with their wives?'). In contrast, the sympathetic master ('Must be patient. No good forcing pace'. 'They're an interesting lot') has a happy marriage or exciting girl friend ('Glad I've got such a devoted wife'. 'To bed. How nice to sleep with Jane. Snuggle up') (pp. 39–40).

Among girls, clear perspectives exist about marital status and classroom performance, which can be summarized in the comment: 'She's married and usually a married one has more understanding'. Another girl suggested to me that married teachers 'tend to be more sort of placid and not get all angry'. Being married is associated with having a happy life outside school. One girl contrasted two 'lonely' spinsters with a married teacher who was 'completely independent, she's married, she's got children, she's happy'.

Indeed I would argue that the unmarried teacher is stigmatized. Goffman (1968b) defines stigma as 'the situation of the individual who is disqualified from full social acceptance' (p. 9). He later elaborates:

> When a stranger is present before us, evidence can arise of his possessing an attribute that makes him different from others in the category of persons (he belongs to). . . . He is thus reduced in our minds from a whole and usual person to a tainted, discounted one. Such an attribute is a stigma. (p. 12)

Goffman stresses that 'an attribute that stigmatizes one type of possessor can confirm the usualness of another'. In other words, one person's stigma is another's badge of normality. The marital status of teachers is one good example. Before the Second World War, when many authorities would not employ married women teachers, a wedding ring would have been a disabling stigma. Now society expects everyone to marry, the absence of the ring is a stigma.

A young woman escapes the stigma of spinsterhood as long as she is thought to be 'having a life of her own outside school'. But the middle-aged spinster is assumed to lack social and sexual life and this has repercussions for the classroom. Goffman argues that stigmatized individuals will be restricted in their actions – there are some things a blind person cannot do without censure. Similarly, there are some things the spinster should not do in her classroom. A teacher like the classicist described in Chapter 1, who keeps her classes firmly concentrated on academic matters, is behaving in an acceptable manner. She may be seen as 'rather shut in by classics and how we're doing', but she will also be seen as efficient, competent, and thus 'a very good teacher'. As one girl said 'you never stop working for a minute. You feel your parents are getting their money's worth'. However, the middle-aged spinster cannot move far from this conventional role. Woe betide the spinster who tries to bring sex into lessons.

Claire Rayner (1966) made this point when writing about sex education for adolescent girls. She noted a great reluctance among them to discuss personal relationships, particularly sexual ones, with unmarried women. As one girl said to her: 'I can't be doing with those lessons they give us at school – the biology teacher is a Miss, so how can she know what she's talking about? And if she does, she shouldn't'. The attempts of one teacher at St Luke's to introduce discussion of love, sex and interpersonal relations had led to her being branded as having 'a dirty mind', 'a one track mind on sex', and even being a 'sex maniac'. When I asked them why they thought this teacher acted as she did, only one girl had any glimmering – the nearest the others came to understanding was to say 'It would do her a great deal of good to get married'.

The middle-aged spinster is therefore stigmatized and caught in a 'double bind'. She is seen as without social or sexual life, and cannot claim to have them without being stigmatized in turn as a 'fallen woman'. Goffman's book includes a discussion of how persons with 'spoiled identity' 'pass' as normal. He writes insightfully about covering many types of stigma from deafness to prostitution. Goffman does not, however, mention spinsterhood as a form of stigma, and therefore suggests no strategies for concealing it. Jean Brodie, of course, compensated for her unmarried state by giving her pupils the tear-jerking account of her true love dying on Flanders fields. The average teacher has no such escape. Woods (1979, p. 103) was told by two girls of an incident in which a scuffle had led to one of them being found clad only in her petticoat by two members of staff. The senior mistress had remonstrated with them about their unladylike behaviour – the girls continued:

Kate: Nobody will marry you, said Miss Judge.
Tracey: Oh yeah, Miss Judge sits there'n 'nobody will want to marry you Jones', she said. I said 'Well you ain't married anyway.'

Thus the spinster is caught. She cannot reveal her social life, and without one she is not fully human. This is manageable as long as she sticks to impersonal concerns, but makes references to the personal impossible. Pupils will accept a definition of the situation as impersonal and instrumental, but not personal and emotional.

Institutional status

Finally, a word needs to be said about institutional status as it affects classroom life. The head or deputy may have an aura of authority which carries into the classroom, as may the teacher who has an informal position in the school. Unfortunately we lack data on these points, although Richardson's (1973) work bears on it. She described how a deputy head, though still teaching history, came to be regarded as a 'guest artist' in the history department: 'by implication already out of touch with the realities of the classroom' (p. 221). Such a feeling among a teacher's colleagues could create all kinds of problems for her in the classroom, but unfortunately Richardson ignores teacher-pupil contacts, so we do not know if the emotion carried over or not. Bullivant's (1978) study suggests that boys judge staff less by institutional status and more by classroom skills of the kind outlined above. He said:

> there is a close correlation between the disruptive class and the boys' apparent perceptions of the teaching competence of the staff member taking it. Even where a master holds a senior position . . . he is judged on class performance. (p. 47)

Private lives and guilty knowledge

Pupils may perceive teachers more or less favourably on the basis of idiosyncratic features of their private lives. At St Luke's (a highly academic school) the status of the university which had granted a teacher's degree figured in the pupils' perspective ('She got her degree in —— from Edinburgh and everyone knows what the —— department is like there – anyone can get a degree there'). A top-stream student interviewed by Metz (1978, p. 80) was obviously using similar criteria to the St

Luke's girls when he said none of the staff were intelligent or they would have better jobs than teaching! The election of one teacher's husband as an FRS increased her prestige. In the Orthodox Jewish school observed by Bullivant (1978, p. 48) reputation as a Hebrew scholar is important, and rabbis have higher status than lay staff. Less intellectual pupils would use less academic criteria – such as 'masculinity', or leisure activities.

Pupils do not, normally, have access to 'guilty knowledge' about their staff. Where they gain access to confidential material on the teacher's private life, it is specially potent because the access is illegitimate. The following example shows this vividly. In the 1960s, when sociology was a rare subject in schools and jobs for sociology graduates in teaching correspondingly scarce, the girls at one convent found out that their young sociology teacher had been the nude pin-up in the centrefold of a famous 'girlie' magazine. This information, calculated to appal the convent authorities, gave the pupils considerable power over the mistress!

The two free schools studied by Swidler (1979) stand out as unusual precisely because the teacher's private lives were opened up to students. At Group High (a white, elite free school):

> Some classes . . . consisted largely of personal exchange. Alice, the teacher, described dilemmas in her love life, her own attitude towards marriage and children and her feelings about being a woman. (p. 59)

Similarly at the black free school (Ethnic High) a teacher called Raymond:

> usually organized each class by asking students for personal experiences . . . He also reminisced freely about his own life . . . (p. 59)

Once teachers had opened up their private lives, students were often critical of them. Thus a teacher at Ethnic High, Gloria, was told that her child was 'a monster', and that pupils felt he was so badly behaved they had to smack him. (Her child was at school with her – another sign of an unusually 'open' school). Another consequence of making teachers' whole selves public was that staff felt constrained to have exciting private lives. So high-status teachers were those with appropriate life styles, such as the jazz musician, the poet, the actor, the civil rights activist, the feminist. Most successful at Group High was Steve

> who taught psychology and PE . . . was skilled in judo, Tai Chi, gestalt psychology, backpacking and other counter cultural specialities. (p. 67)

The very openness of these staff reveals just how private – that is secret from pupils – most teachers' lives are.

'Sussing out' the teacher

Sussing out the teacher is a continuous process in which all pupils are constantly engaged. One of Gibson's (1973) interviewees describes being on the receiving end of such scrutiny:

> As soon as you come into the classroom you feel the class is weighing you up, and you get the impression that they are weighing you up faster than you are them. It's difficult because a class gets to know a teacher more quickly than a teacher gets to know a class. (p. 58)

Pupils are constantly testing the teacher to see if she can keep order, and whether or not her lessons are going to work. It is also important that they discover what their tasks are, what work they are expected to do. Pupils have to find out what they are supposed to be doing and how little they can get away with. A paper by Beynon and Atkinson is reproduced in Delamont (1984) showing pupils' discovery strategies at work.

The best studies of students sussing out the level and direction of effort required by their teachers has been done in the USA by a team of symbolic interactionists trained by Everett Hughes. This team studied student life at Kansas University medical school (*Boys in White*, Becker *et al.*, 1961) and in the Kansas University undergraduate programme (*Making the Grade*, Becker *et al.*, 1968). These are much the best accounts of how students understand their world, and it is a pity that there is nothing comparable on British schools. (Of course, students are much more articulate about their perspectives and this does make research on them easier and more pleasant.) The Kansas research team first turned their attention to the problem of students' level and direction of effort when faced with medical students who have, in an acute form, a problem which faces all learners:

> Medical students . . . are continuously presented with an enormous and, in any practical sense, unlimited amount of material to learn. Though students and faculty agree that the criterion for choosing what to learn should be relevance to medical practice, there is enough disagreement and uncertainty among the faculty as to what is relevant so that the student is *never presented with a clear directive to guide him in his own studies.* (Hughes *et al.*, 1958, emphasis mine)

The researchers found gradual changes in the medical students' perspectives on work as they became aware of the load. When studying the pre-clinical sciences (anatomy, physiology, etc.), the students begin with the idea that everything they are taught is important. This initial perspective is soon challenged when they find it impossible to learn everything and is replaced by a new perspective: learning everything important. This brings its own difficulty – deciding what is important. Two solutions were found. Some students decided they would concentrate on learning what they will need in medical practice. Others opt for learning what is necessary to pass the exams. For this group, important facts are those stressed by faculty and therefore likely to turn up on the exam papers. Both groups of students develop strategies for cutting down the work in accordance with their perspectives, which are often contrary to the wishes of the faculty. As the exams loom, all the students concentrate on the main objective: passing the exams and staying in medical school.

Becker and his colleagues applied the same techniques to the undergraduates at Kansas University, and although their approach works better on the medical students because of their isolated, self-contained world, the perspectives of the ordinary undergraduates have more in common with those of school pupils and therefore are analysed in more detail here. At Kansas, as in most American colleges, students do a variety of courses in different subjects and are assessed at frequent intervals by essays, tests, quizzes and full examinations. Their work (and often their performance in class) is graded from A to F, and then a Grade Point Average is calculated to measure their performance across all their subjects. The Grade Point Average (GPA) at Kansas can range from 3.0 (all As) to −1.0 (all Fs) and a student with a GPA of zero or worse is likely to be thrown out of college.

A student's GPA rules his life. Those on scholarships need a GPA of about 2.5 if they are to keep their money. Students are not allowed to hold any office on campus without a C average. One popular form of living arrangement, the fraternity or sorority (a co-operative residence and club), demands a 'reasonable' average from members. The 'better' the fraternity the higher the GPA demanded will be. All these pressures interconnect, for a student with bad grades is not only in danger of being thrown out of university, his social, political, athletic and domestic activities are certain to be affected. Thus one girl told the researchers:

> That boy is going to flunk out. You can see why I won't go out with him. I don't want to go out with a boy who might be flunking out. (p. 119)

The all-embracing and bureaucratic nature of the GPA 'obsession' is alien to the British audience. The world of continual, weekly, multiple-choice tests on one or two set texts seems a long way from the leisurely British school system. However, the underlying dilemmas for the students are the same. The Kansas undergraduates have a more explicit, and systematic, perspective, but it is fundamentally similar to that expressed in a more fragmentary form by British school pupils.

Instructors' idiosyncrasies

Students, for example, recognize that: 'Instructors vary greatly in the number and kinds of demands they make for academic performance' (p. 65) and so they suspect that 'every class will be different'. This expectation of teacher idiosyncrasy is common among pupils too – hence the sizing up of new teachers described above. As one girl at St Luke's, Georgina, put it:

> Some people, like Mrs Flodden, like you to be very keen – always wanting you to do projects, while others don't mind as long as you do what's on the syllabus.

Becker and his co-workers contrast various ways in which the students organize themselves to discover what the instructor's requirements are. They contrast the formal, written regulations, which specify the minimum standard, with the hidden curriculum which has to be discovered and consists of finding out, for example, whether marks are deducted for spelling mistakes. As Olivia complained to me, of Mrs Linnaeus:

> She has to have everything perfect, very hard marker – if you have a few scorings out in your essay she gives you a mark off.

Students must also work out what is required in the classroom. Some teachers demand only a passive audience, while others expect participation in discussion. Participation has its own rules. One Kansas lecturer demanded that his students answer in 'complete, grammatically correct sentences'. In addition, students have to discover how they will be assessed. Multiple-choice and short-answer quizzes need detailed memorization, while longer thematic essays demand thematic learning.

Gaining good marks

Discovering how grades will be awarded is only half the battle. The students still have to obtain good marks. The researchers describe various student strategies, legitimate, semi-legitimate and illegitimate. (The latter are more entertaining to read about!) Students are seen calling on the experience of their fellow students. The fraternity provides help for students in difficulties.

> For instance, in chemistry we have a fellow who is majoring in chemistry who is very good in Chem I and Chem II particularly, so he will have review sessions with the boys that are taking that course . . . of course he's very sharp on what kinds of questions they'll ask on the examinations. . . . (p. 104)

As St Luke's I found a very similar practice. In physics, all the girls told me that only one girl, Charmian, understood the lessons, and in practical lessons I frequently observed girls checking their work with her and getting her to explain things to them. She ran remedial tutorials from the back of the lab.

At Kansas, Becker found students trying to get themselves good reputations by gaining 'brownie points' or 'apple-polishing'. (We lack vivid equivalents of these terms in Britain. Brownie points derive from a bowdlerization of 'brown-nosing', for which 'bum-licking' is the only English equivalent I can raise. Apple-polishing derives from the idea of bringing an apple for the teacher.) One Kansas student describes how he cultivates his lecturers, dropping into their offices and chatting them up about their interests. Allied to this was the common belief that it paid to agree with the faculty's opinions.

> It just doesn't pay to disagree with them, there's no point in it. The thing to do is find out what they want you to say and tell them that. (p. 100)

Similar sentiments were expressed at St Luke's. One girl, Monica, told me 'I make it my business to get on with teachers', and a friend of hers, Katherine, describes Monica's strategy:

> (Good pupils) pay attention in class the whole time. Suck up – clean boards, etcetera – make suggestions. Monica did that to Mrs Bruce, and she absolutely adores her.

Katherine herself eschewed Monica's plotting: 'I don't try to be liked – it's up to them whether they like me as I am or not'. This resulted in Katherine's unpopularity with staff, for as Caitlin explained to me, Katherine 'has her own opinions and lets them know'. This was a recipe for disaster in the eyes of most pupils. Of course girls also recognized that not all teachers responded to the same strategies. Claire told me:

> Some teachers can tell when you're trying to be one of their little pets – like going up and cleaning the blackboard when you're not told to – some are taken in by that and some aren't.

Bargaining

Other gambits reported from Kansas include arguing with the lecturers about the marks to get them raised (as Werthman, 1963, also found) and different kinds of cheating – from handing in work written by other successful students to cribbing from published materials. Dishonesty did not seem prevalent at St Luke's, although it is commonly reported from lower-stream boys (Hargreaves, 1967; Willis, 1977) and girls (Meyenn, 1980).

Bargaining for marks did go on however, and went hand in hand with discovering how they would be awarded. The best example I collected centred round a geography test. On the third Wednesday of my fieldwork I went to the top geography set. The lesson opened with Mrs Hill being buttonholed by Jill with an involved query about fish farming. Then Mrs Hill called the class to order and announced a test on 'all Scotland' for the following week, giving them the rest of that lesson to revise for it. My notes continue:

> A chorus of groans, protests and objections breaks out – dies away – to be replaced by questions on the nature of the test.
> Jackie: What type of questions? Short answer or essay?
> Mrs Hill: Short answer mostly.
> Jill: Why do we have to have tests all the time?
> Lorraine: Will we be asked to draw anything?
> Karen: Will it be on the board, or are you going to read them out?
> Mrs Hill: (Says she'll read them out, and tells them they may have to draw. Then tells them to quieten down or she'll go on to the next topic – Newcastle).

The girls were silenced, and the rest of the period consisted of revision, with girls asking questions about geography as they found points they were not sure of.

The following week I watched the test, which consisted of short answer questions read aloud, such as 'Name two coal-fired power stations in Scotland'. Once it was over the girls swapped papers and marked their neighbour's script.

Mrs Hill: (Announces a firm marking schedule and says there are to be no arguments about it. Then starts asking round the class to get the answers. . .)

Later:

Mrs Hill: Right, now what do we call the area of fertile farmland which includes Perthshire?

(Evelyn is giggling hysterically. Mrs H. asks her what the matter is, but Evelyn does not, or cannot manage to answer. Mrs H. sends her out of the room, takes her test paper away from Angela, and makes Angela and Karen swap).

Jackie: The golden girdle.

Karen bursts out laughing, and Mrs H. asks her what is funny.

Karen: Angela has got 'golden griddle', not 'girdle'.

Mrs H. laughs, and the whole class dissolves into laughter.

Mrs H: She can have half a mark for ingenuity. Get Evelyn back in will you?

A chorus of protests about the half mark – for the schedule had stated 'no half marks'.

Mrs H. ignores protests. Tells Evelyn she can see why it was funny, but she should have explained why she was laughing. They go on. Another question asked for 'the industries of Glasgow after the American War of Independence'. After the right answers have been given, Karen raises her hand and is asked what she wants. . .

Karen: I had 'the slave trade'. Does that count?

Mrs H: That's not an industry.

Karen: Well, for modern Scotland we've got 'tourism' as an industry – if tourists are an industry surely slaves are too?

Mrs H. gives in and lets her have a half mark too. Another chorus of 'Not fair' breaks out and is silenced . . . The next question deals with the potato crop, and Mrs H. says that only 'early potatoes' will do for the mark – just 'potatoes' won't do. A chorus of protests demand half a mark for 'potatoes', but Mrs Hill refuses and is adamant.

Here we can see bargaining as astute as anything reported from Kansas. A similar incident is reported by Bullivant (1978, pp. 122–3), showing hard pupil-bargaining for marks. Such behaviours are an integral part of the role for many pupils.

The pupil's life

Thus, all successful pupils must learn to size up teachers and the tasks they set, and then work out strategies to cope with the tasks. The traditional pupil role is a subservient one, in which the main duties are to follow the teacher's lead. Where such leads are ambiguous, or unpopular, pupils may reject their role and combine together to disrupt the classroom process. The more the pupils combine, the less the teacher is able to impose her definition of the situation upon them. High-status pupils will have different attributes in different schools, classes or streams, but the high-status pupil can mobilize more support from her fellows either for or against the staff.

The last two chapters have introduced the teacher and the pupils, the next shows how the protagonists react to each other and interact in the classroom.

5 Let battle commence: strategies for the classroom

Chapter 2 set the classroom in its context, while Chapters 3 and 4 introduced the teacher and the pupils. These chapters presented material on the ways in which teachers and pupils arrive at classroom encounters: their hopes and fears, beliefs about their roles and duties, and their perspectives on each other. This chapter examines what happens when they meet.

Classroom encounters

It is essential to separate two types of teacher-pupil encounter. When a teacher faces a new class for the first time, both parties have ideas about what classroom life is like in general, but new rules have to be established for the new relationship. This *initial encounter* can be contrasted with a *routine* meeting, between a teacher and a class who know each other. In the routine situation some rules are known, and negotiations take account of earlier encounters, as the 'strawberries' incident given in Chapter 2 showed vividly.

In many ways it would be easier to do research into initial encounters because the investigator is in the same knowledge state as the participants. The routine encounter, because it draws on previous meetings between that teacher and that class, is less accessible to researchers. In practice, we have studies of routine encounters but not of initial ones. Because the first meeting of a teacher and class is problematic, observers rarely gain access to it, but concentrate on studying established relationships. The main source of material on initial encounters is that vigorous tradition of educational writing: the autobiography or 'non-fiction novel' popularized by Blishen. This *genre* is discussed by Whiteside and Mathieson (1971) and is used by Hargreaves (1972) to illustrate the establishment and maintenance of order. Here I use an example by a New Zealander, Bream (1970), who writes amusingly of her first year in a rough technical high school and her struggles with H3C, a class of low-ability girls. She describes her first encounter with H3C:

I brought them into my room, and when all were seated the class and I looked at each other with interest . . .

'Are you going to be our form teacher?' asked a little plump girl . . .

'You know quite well that I am,' I said coldly. 'The First Assistant has just . . . told you so.'

The girl smiled at me. 'I'm Denise,' she said.

'How long are you going to stay?' asked her neighbour . . .

'Where did you come from, Mrs Bream?' asked another girl.

'Do you like this school?'

'Do you like teaching?'

'Do you think it's fair that girls aren't allowed to wear nail polish?'

'You are so, if it's clear, Miss Ferguson said.'

'She said natural, and mine's natural, and I can show her the label if she likes, but she still made me take it off . . .'

I began the lesson. 'I shall be taking you for English, as you know. So take out your English textbooks. Well, where *are* they? Weren't you issued with any?' There were five textbooks in the room.

'We thought you might do something else.' 'We didn't know we were having English.' 'I've lost mine.' 'Mine's in my locker.' 'I've lent mine to someone.' 'Can we do geography this period?' 'Can we have a debate?' 'Mr Bunting used to tell us about India'. 'Have you been to India?' . . .

Mrs Bream sets them some work, which fills up the English lesson.

> The bell rang, and I took in their papers.
> 'We stay here, don't we?' they asked.
> 'Yes', I said. 'We do social studies this period. Take out your social study books.'
> They gasped at this monstrous suggestion. 'We have a rest first' . . . 'Do you?' I asked feebly.
> They did. (Bream, 1970, pp. 35–9)

Here we can see three separate stages of negotiation quite clearly. At first the girls try to find out about their new teacher and/or start a discussion on school discipline to find out where she stands. Bream is already wary of such feelers after an encounter the previous day. She had asked a class to tell her about the school, and they replied *en masse*: 'It's a rotten dump'. Bream had been forced to reject this definition, saying feebly 'You mustn't say that. It's a fine school'. This reply brought gales of laughter.

Bream had learnt enough to avoid H3C's skirmishing, and redefines the situation as an English class. This definition, too, is challenged, albeit in a ritualized way, and Bream avoids being drawn into a discussion of possible reasons why it might not be English. The third challenge is accepted, in that she allows the girls their rest. They convince her, by their unanimity (and non-verbal cues) that they are genuine in their demand for a rest – it is taken for granted – and Bream has to accept their definition. The reader follows Bream through many encounters, and can observe the negotiated areas growing and the 'no man's land' diminishing.

Finally, we can see her successful strategies revealed for us. The deputy head has ticked Bream off because the chairs in her form room had not been lifted on to the desks one night. Bream wants to hold an inquest:

> If I said, 'Who took down the chairs?', no one would answer.

If I said 'Did you put down the chairs?', all of them would answer. They would reply that of course they didn't, they wouldn't do that, it must have been those girls in the next room, or the caretaker, or some boys . . . I had no doubt . . . that only H3C would have taken them down. '*Why?*', I said finally, 'tell me just *why* you took all the chairs off the desks last night?' (p. 223)

The girls decide that Bream knows they did it, and explain.

Mrs Bream has obviously learnt how to handle H3C. She can put forward a definition of the situation which is acceptable to them, and realizes that certain questions will be interpreted as accusations while others will produce answers. She can sound more knowledgeable than she is, and avoid pitfalls. She can also manage to teach them English when she wants to. An observer visiting her class would not find a restrained academic atmosphere, but would see a negotiated order susceptible to study with systematic schedules. A working relationship exists.

Stephen Ball (1980) is one sociologist who has looked at initial encounters between teachers and strange classes. He accepts that teachers are often reluctant to have researchers around during the earliest days of the school year and then goes on:

but the reasons for the teacher's reluctance are exactly the reasons why the researcher should be there. These earlier encounters are of crucial significance not only for understanding what comes later but in actually providing for what comes later.

Ball then focuses on what he terms the 'process of establishment' which he defines as:

an exploratory interaction process involving teacher and pupils during their initial encounters in the classroom through which a more or less permanent, repeated and highly predictable pattern of relationships and interactions emerges.

Ball analyses two sets of data on the process of establishment: some from a comprehensive school introducing mixed-ability teaching and some from student teachers on school practice.

These data reveal two stages in the pupils' treatment of strange teachers.

> the first is a passive, and in a sense, purely observational stage . . . After this the second stage is embarked upon, which usually involves at least some pupils in being 'real horrible' . . .

In other words, the pupils first make observations to get a series of hypotheses about the kind of teacher they are facing, and then test their hypotheses. Ball argues that pupils use the results of these testing sessions to guide their future attitudes and behaviours. For the rest of their careers with that teacher they will face a multitude of decisions about whether to obey each instruction, command or order the teacher issues or not, and they can only make these decisions if they can predict how the teacher will react. Ball says that the pupils' anticipation of the teacher's likely response enables them:

> to weigh up the amount of satisfaction to be obtained from the commission of a 'deviant' act against the dissatisfaction likely to be involved in the teacher's response to it, if any. This may in fact account for pupils' often stated preference for 'strict' teachers. Strictness usually also provides for a highly structured and therefore a highly predictable situational definition.

The second (testing) stage, the pupils' decisions, and the part played by violence in the establishment process are the subjects of a paper by Beynon and Delamont (1984). Beynon found eleven-year-old boys deliberately provoking teachers because, as Robert told him: 'I just wanted to find out which teachers were hard and which soft, because I was going to get down to work then'. Here Robert makes a clear and somewhat coldblooded statement about his strategy for settling into his new school. In an interview he describes fluently how he deliberately used another boy – David – to find out about the teachers in his new secondary school. He sat next to David (a boy who caused endless disruption in class) and used David to test the strength of the teachers. Robert believed that he needed to discover what the staff were like and 'David found all those things out for us'. Not only did David test the teachers for the whole class: 'being with him was like being on holiday' because he caused so many upsets. After four weeks the boys were given tests and Robert went into an academic form, 1W, while David stayed in a low form. Robert had had a very successful settling in period.

The staff at Robert and David's school – a boys' comprehensive which Beynon calls Victoria Road – saw David as a ringleader in troublemaking and Robert as his innocent dupe. Robert's account of the relationship was quite different. The researcher (John Beynon) asked:

Did Kingsey have a hold, an influence, over you? Did he use you?

Robert: O no, I used him!

J.B.: Meaning?

R.: Well I mucked about with Kingsey because I wanted to, not because he forced me or anything like that. We mucked around together and it was fun. But I made sure I did my work as well, whereas I could see he wasn't doing anything . . . . I let him copy because I knew it wasn't going to make any difference, he wasn't going to take it in because he hadn't done the work for himself.

Pupil behaviour of this kind is one reason why experienced teachers argue that staff must start by behaving strictly, and ease up later in the year (if at all). These boys wanted to know which teachers were 'hard', as this quote shows:

. . . in that first week we were messing around like anything and he took us back behind the hut after a lesson and we knew that if he was soft that he would just tell us off, and if he was hard he'd hit us, and he hit us! He smacked Kingsey against the wall and kicked us both up the backside . . . that's how we found out about Mr New.

These pupils have already had six years of schooling and know what is expected of pupils. Studies by David Hamilton (1977, reprinted in Delamont, 1984) and by Mary Willes (1981) have focused on how very young children first learn the pupil role. Many features of classrooms occupied by older children which are taken for granted are seen, through the eyes of five-year-olds as problematic. For example, Hamilton (1977, p. 45) shows Mrs Robertson explicitly teaching children how to say 'Good Morning, Mrs Robertson' in chorus: something 'learnt' within the first week of school. As more and more research is done by practising teachers (Nixon, 1981), more data on initial encounters will become available. Analyses are needed of how different schools try to socialize new pupils, and how the protagonists in classrooms come to construct shared meanings, establish rules, and learn to live together in a joint world. The ORACLE project (Galton and Willcocks, 1983) allows comparison of the settling in process for new pupils in six different schools. The research team found staff putting emphasis on teaching the rules of their particular subject and their classroom, while the pupils 'tested' staff in ways similar to those described by Ball and Beynon. Until we have more such research it is difficult to say more about the establishment of classroom norms, and so this chapter is concentrated on the research which does exist, that of established classroom relationships.

Routine encounters

This book is about classroom constants – those features of life in classrooms which shine through the pettifogging detail of the multifarious schedules and category systems. This means examining the conceptions of teaching which underlie the various research techniques as well as assimilating their findings. In this chapter a selection of the main findings on teacher and pupil actions from category systems and ethnography is presented.

The research tradition of systematic observation becomes visible again in this chapter, because teacher-pupil interaction is the central concern. Systematic observers are not concerned with the type of material presented in Chapters 2, 3 and 4 whereas ethnographers are, but both groups study classroom interaction. A fully summary of all research findings would be enormous, so the chapter presents a few general principles which have been established across dozens of different studies. The organizing concept is that of teacher and pupil *strategies* (Woods, 1980a and 1980b). Both teachers and pupils are seen as engaging in negotiations, and both are seen as having 'typical', 'normal', 'taken-for-granted' strategies which they adopt so regularly that it is easy to miss them altogether. Teacher strategies are considered first.

Teacher strategies

Teachers talk

The teacher's first strategy is to impose her definition of the situation by talking most of the time. So teachers talk. And not only do they talk – they talk a great deal. It is hard for any of us to think seriously about this proposition because teaching and talking are so closely bound up in our culture. If you doubt this, try to imagine a silent teacher.

> I was at this time teaching two sixth forms – an upper stream set in their second sixth-form year . . . and a lower stream set in the first sixth-form year. . . . It was with the younger and lower set that I am here concerned. They had been very difficult from the start . . . one morning when the class was expecting a double lesson introducing them to Jane Austen – a name most of them despised from a distance – I came in, sat at a desk at the side of the room, and said nothing.
>
> The class fell silent after a while. Noticing that Ezekiel was absent, someone shouted mockingly that I would not start without him. Deacon made a flagrantly outrageous suggestion. I possessed my soul in patience. Ezekiel came in, sensed the unusual atmosphere, and sat down looking puzzled. Still nothing. After ten minutes, and when the strain was becoming unendurable, English jumped up, red in the face, and yelled at me, 'Are you going to start us or not? If not, I'm going' . . . Fenn suddenly turned on me, and spat out with real venom, 'Number one madman here is *him*'. English slammed the door and was gone. (Stuart, 1969, pp. 48–50)

This is a melodramatic incident, but it shows what happens when cultural assumptions are violated. The silent teacher has abrogated her role. So the teacher must talk – but does she have to talk so much? Two-thirds of the time teachers and pupils spend in the classroom someone is talking. Two-thirds of that talking is done by the teacher.

Flanders (1970), the pioneer of interaction analysis research (whose category system is shown in Figure 5.1), suggests that the typical American classroom has 68 per cent teacher talk, 20 per cent pupil talk, and 12 per cent is lost in 'silence and

Figure 5.1

Flanders's Interaction Analysis Categories (FIAC)

	1.	Accepts feeling
	2.	Praises or encourages
	3.	Accepts or uses ideas of pupils
Teacher talk	4.	Asks questions
	5.	Lecturing
	6.	Giving directions
	7.	Criticizing or justifying authority
Pupil talk	8.	Pupil-talk – response
	9.	Pupil-talk – initiation
Silence	10.	Silence or confusion

The observer codes classroom talk into one of these ten categories every three seconds. A 40-minute lesson produces 800 tallies. (Adapted from Flanders, 1970, p. 34)

confusion'. Using his system, the observer would expect to tally 68 per cent of the lesson in categories 1 through 7, 20 per cent in categories 8 and 9, and to 'lose' the rest in category 10. The average American teaching nine-year-olds talks 53 per cent of the time; teaching twelve-year-olds 61 per cent; and doing maths with thirteen-years-olds 70 per cent. American teachers certainly talk a great deal.

These figures could be telling us something about American schools, or about Flanders's category system, rather than something about the basic nature of classroom interaction. However, research reported from all over the world shows a similar pattern: in India, Belgium, Iraq, South America and New Zealand the teacher keeps on talking. Britain is no exception. Politics teachers in Scotland talk 77 per cent of the time! (Morrison, 1973). Wragg (1973) found that the pupils' share of classroom talk fell throughout secondary school from 32 per cent in the first year to 23 per cent in the fifth and sixth years. Wragg's sample of student teachers talked for between 73 and 81 per cent of their lesson time in all subjects but English and modern languages (approximately 60 per cent). These were student teachers, and one could argue that experienced staff would show different figures, but there is no evidence of this. I studied established teachers in two Scottish girls' schools, and found that the average teacher was talking 70 per cent of the time, with the history and geography staff talking 80 per cent and more!

Nor are these figures about teacher talk a mere artefact of the FIAC system which, by focusing on teacher talk, highlights it. A completely different systematic observation schedule, devised by Deanne Boydell, the Teacher Record, has been used for over ten years in British junior schools, and was a central research instrument of the ORACLE project (Galton, Simon and Croll, 1980, p. 17). This system, designed for use in the contemporary junior school, is more complex than FIAC, but it, too, reveals the centrality of teacher talk in classroom life. Figure 5.2 shows, in summary form, the main categories.

Using this system the researcher makes a coding every 25 seconds, recording not only what the teacher is doing, but

Figure 5.2

The observation categories of the teacher record

Conversation	Silence

Conversation	Silence
Questions	Silent interaction
Task	Gesturing
Q1 recalling facts	Showing
Q2 offering ideas, solutions (closed)	Marking
Q3 offering ideas, solutions (open)	Waiting
Task supervision	Story
Q4 referring to task supervision	Reading
Routine	Not observed
Q5 referring to routine matter	Not coded
Statements	No interaction
Task	Adult interaction
S1 of facts	Visiting pupil
S2 of ideas, problems	Not interacting
Task supervision	Out of room
S3 telling child what to do	
S4 praising work or effort	Audience
S5 feedback on work or effort	Composition
Routine	Activity
S6 providing information, directions	
S7 providing feedback	
S8 of critical control	
S9 of small talk	

whom she is doing it with. Using this coding system the ORACLE research team found (Galton, Simon and Croll, 1980, p. 85) that teachers in junior school classes were interacting with pupils 79 per cent of the time, and this 79 per cent was made up of 12 per cent 'Questioning', 22 per cent 'Silent interactions', and 45 per cent 'Statements'. These figures, collected in a very different way from FIAC in different kinds of classroom, reveal the same basic pattern: 60 per cent teacher talk. Flanders merely shares with other people in Western society the assumption that teaching and talking are synonymous. Researchers do not challenge this taken-for-granted norm. Instead they build their systems round it. Research only centres on pupil speech when radical changes in teaching methods are under scrutiny. In normal classroom research the belief that teacher talk is the major feature of the discourse both in quantity and quality is never challenged. In one sense this assumption is 'correct', because teachers and pupils share it. Most classrooms *are* dominated by teacher talk. Studies of tape recordings show teachers speaking three or four times as much as all the pupils put together (Bellack *et al.*, 1966).

So far this discussion has centred on conventional 'chalk and talk' classrooms. It could be argued that 'open plan' classes would show a different pattern. In fact, teachers talk just as much in open classrooms. Of course there is more pupil talk, because pupils talk to each other, but the teacher is rarely silent. She moves around, and different pupils receive different utterances – but she still talks a hell of a lot. The transcripts of recordings made in open classrooms by Walker and Adelman (1975b) and Edwards and Furlong (1978) show this vividly. Informal classrooms are different from conventional ones in many ways, but the overall rule – that teachers talk a great deal – holds good.

Of course, just talking would not necessarily achieve acceptance of the teacher's perspectives by the pupils. She has to talk to some point. Belinda complained to me of Miss Knox: 'She was dreadful . . . she goes on about her own life and not about general history at all, and then she wonders why we fail the exams'. Volume of speech is not enough – it must have content. This gives us our second rule:

Teachers teach

The teacher defines what constitutes knowledge by concentrating on direct imposition of her version of it. She imposes her definition of subjects by direct lecture and questioning of pupils, playing down other perspectives. This also sounds too obvious to be worth stating. Earlier in this book we have seen evidence that teachers rate instruction as an important part of their duties, and that pupils expect to be taught. However, such expectations would not necessarily mean that teachers actually instructed anybody. We all pay lip service to things we never do, or have unfulfilled expectations from life. However, the research available does suggest that teachers do instruct their pupils – or rather that they spend a lot of time on academic content. This is particularly true in secondary schools, where the proportion of time spent in academic material rises with the age of the pupils.

The proposition that teachers teach is as difficult to examine as the statement that they talk. We expect to find teachers engaged in instruction – that is transferring knowledge from various sources to their pupils. Just as the emphasis on teacher speech is taken for granted by most classroom researchers, so too there is an unchallenged assumption that teachers are involved in cognitive transactions. Researchers have taken for granted the idea that classroom interaction is largely cognitive. Whole systems have been developed to focus on this aspect alone. (See, for example, the Science Teacher Observation Schedule of Eggleston, Galton and Jones, 1976; and Gallagher, 1970.)

Flanders's (1970) system gives us a handy way of measuring how much of the teacher's speech is devoted to lecturing and questioning the pupils about the academic subject of the lesson – the content cross ratio (CCR) devised from categories 4 and 5 of his system. The higher the CCR the more concentration on academic material there is. Flanders suggests a 'mythical national average' of 55 per cent for the USA, but adds that the figure will be higher for certain academic subjects in secondary schools. In Britain Wragg found the average CCR rising from 43 per cent in the first year of secondary school to 63 per cent in the sixth (with certain subject variations). In two Scottish schools the average in the fourth year was 52 per cent. Other research reports show a similar concentration by the teacher on the subject matter of lessons. The ORACLE project (Galton, Simon and Croll, 1980, pp. 86–90) found 57 per cent of teacher talk was questions or statements. Among teacher questions 85 per cent were task-related, and among statements 73 per cent were. However the data are collected, it appears that at least 50 per cent of the teacher's talk is teaching in the narrowest sense: lecturing and questioning pupils about what she perceives as the academic content of the lesson.

The other half

Chapter 3 looked at the strength of the teacher's control over knowledge and the central place such control has in the definition of the teacher's role. This dominance is reflected in the high CCR reported from research with FIAC and from other projects. However, this direct imposition only accounts for about half the teacher's utterances. The other half includes the indirect imposition of her definition of the situation (or rather her attempts to impose her perspective by indirect means); her explicit disciplinary and management moves, and much of her reaction to pupil contributions. In other words, many of the most problematic aspects of the teaching role (discipline, organization, checking for comprehension, and ensuring that her control over content is secure) occupy only half her speech time.

The teacher's strategy is firstly to make her expectations for the classroom explicit, and to state and restate them frequently. Her attempts at controlling both content and pupil behaviour are made, in the first instance, by direct statements of her expected standards.

It is revealing to break down the 50 per cent of the teacher's talk not spent in direct instruction and discover how much of it consists of explicit disciplining and controlling moves. Hughes's (1959) work on elementary school teachers in the USA showed that over 40 per cent of teaching acts fell into what she called the 'controlling' category – teachers rarely expanded student ideas or responded personally to them. This gross figure can be set into a more realistic framework by examining Boydell's (1974) work in British primary schools. She found that the teachers spent only 25 per cent of their time on organization and discipline. However, because those utterances tended to be public they reached all children, which many of the other utterances did not. Thus, for any specific pupil, two out of five teacher utterances *heard* were organizational and disciplinary. Research in informally run classrooms has to take account of these two perspectives – what the teacher's talk consists of, and how it is received by different pupils. The later work with Boydell's schedules done by Galton, Simon and Croll (1980, p. 89) in over a hundred classrooms found similar proportions.

In the more formal secondary classes studied by Flanders and Wragg it is clear that the half of the teacher's speech not in the CCR is approximately equally divided between explicitly controlling and organizing pupils and personal interaction with them. Thus we can summarize that *at least a quarter of the teacher's talk is designed to organize and discipline pupils by explicit statement*. Therefore at least 75 per cent of teacher talk is concerned with explicit statement of the teacher's definition of the appropriate behaviour and content of classroom life.

These first three strategies suggest that much teacher behaviour is in accordance with the role expectancies held for them by their pupils and society at large. They attempt to control their classes and then to teach them something. However, such global generalizations only tell us about the teacher's strategies in the broadest terms, and more analysis is needed of the *minutiae* of their attempts at controlling and instruction. However, before turning to the finer detail we need to look at the pupils' overall strategy in relation to that of the teacher.

Pupil strategies

The pupils' first strategy is to find out what the teacher wants and give it to her – assuming that they can see a pay-off for themselves, in terms of grades, eventual jobs, or peace and quiet. When there is no discernible benefit to be had by giving the teacher what she wants, 'disruptive behaviour' is likely to become the major strategy.

In one way we all know what pupils do because we have all been on the receiving end of teaching processes. Oddly enough, however, we have relatively little research on pupils' classroom strategies against which to test our subjective reminiscences. Thus, only nine of the 99 systems in Simon and Boyer's (1974)

122

anthology focus on pupils, and these are all designed for use in non-traditional classrooms. In part this is because pupil talk, in the conventional classroom, is a rare phenomenon. If there is 70 per cent teacher talk and 20 per cent pupil talk in the 'typical' 40-minute period the teacher has 25 minutes and the pupils eight. This is not a great deal of data to analyse!

It is possible to make generalizations about the sum total of pupil talk – about overall pupil strategies. However, the pupils are not just a group, they are individuals, and any sensitive study ought to look for ways in which the differing perspectives of individuals and sub-groups are reflected in different classroom strategies. This is, of course, exceptionally time-consuming when the classroom is formal, because so few data are available on each pupil in each lesson. If there are eight minutes of pupil talk in a period, and that subject is taught for five lessons a week, there are forty minutes of pupil talk in that subject per week. In a class of twenty that gives each pupil two minutes per week to talk aloud. In a class of forty each pupil has only one minute! (Of course, these minutes are not equally divided between the pupils – some use more than others, as we shall see below.) It is, however, hardly surprising that there is not a large research literature on how pupils use their minute! A systematic schedule that coded only public pupil talk would leave two-thirds of the observer's time unused – such systems would be a form of conspicuous consumption of precious observer time.

Public talk in the formal classroom is one of the ways pupils can test their definition of the situation against the teacher's, as the extracts from Bream (1970) and the St Luke's geography lesson show. Two minutes per week do not give the pupil much scope for testing her definitions against others. The pupil in an informal class can match her conceptions against those of other pupils – but she too gets little chance to test them against the teacher's. Boydell (1974) found that the pupil in the informal primary class gets two minutes of academic interaction with the teacher in an hour. Galton, Simon and Croll (1980, pp. 60–1) report the same finding as follows:

> while the teacher is interacting with pupils for most of a
> teaching session, the individual pupil interacts with the

teacher for only a small proportion of this time. In a one hour session . . . this amounts to a total of nine minutes, 29 seconds . . . the bulk of this interaction is experienced by the child when the teacher is addressing the class as a whole . . .

The authors remark on the tiny amount of individual attention any one pupil gets: one minute and 23 seconds per hour as an individual, plus 54 seconds as a member of a small group. No systematic plotting of this kind has been carried out in informal secondary classrooms, but the overall figures are unlikely to be very different.

However, just as the teacher talks more than all the pupils in both formal and informal classrooms, so too there are pupil strategies in common across both types. Most pupils share a basic strategy of pleasing teacher. They play along with whatever communication style is demanded, assuming that they can discover what it is and accept its reasonableness and pay-off. Different groups of pupils will have different standards of tolerance – the girls studied by Furlong (1976) had very low thresholds of intolerance compared to the boys of Hightown Grammar (Lacey, 1970). In Torode's (1976) work it is clear that the boys cannot discover what their maths master's definition of the situation is – it is not made accessible to them in a rational manner.

In most classrooms, playing the teacher's game means *responding* – that is, answering the teacher's questions, preferably correctly. Bellack (1966) shows this to be the predominant student strategy in the American high school, as do the figures for the Pupil Initiation Ratio (PIR) quoted by Flanders (1970) and Wragg (1973). During my research I developed a set of categories for coding pupil talk which, among other things, divided their contributions into those directly related to the academic content (content-oriented) and those tangential to it. The system was used in 98 lessons, in which I tallied 1,503 content-oriented contributions and only 882 tangential ones. That is, there were twice as many content-oriented utterances as tangential ones. An 'average' lesson had twenty-four pupil contributions, of which fifteen (63 per cent) were content-oriented. Evidence from other studies suggest these proportions are typical of pupils' classroom behaviour.

Thus, the pupils' first strategy is to provide 'correct' – that is, acceptable to the teacher – answers. To do this, they must concentrate on the teacher enough to discover what the right answers are – or are likely to be. Similarly, pupil responses have to be solicited in some way. Unsolicited pupil comments are disruptive in most classrooms. Most pupil responses are answers to teacher questions, and teacher questions tell pupils a lot about what the teacher wants. Accordingly, the next section looks in some detail at how teachers frame questions, before pupil responses are analysed in depth.

Teacher questions

Teachers' questioning strategies have been the focus of several research projects, some of which are discussed in more detail elsewhere in this series (Stubbs, 1983). One important study is Bellack (1966), who separated four types of speech move: structuring, soliciting, responding and reacting. The researchers found that teacher and pupil roles in classroom discourse were well defined. Teachers initiated (i.e. soliciting and structuring) and pupils responded. Perhaps surprisingly, little time is spent structuring (only 13 per cent). Therefore most of the teacher's defining of the situation must take place via her solicitations (which occupy 20–40 per cent of the dialogue). Many of these solicitations will be questions, and the form these take can be analysed further.

Barnes (1971) analysed tape recordings of a small number of lessons in the first year of a comprehensive school. In all subjects but science 'factual' questions predominated. That is, teachers asked questions which demanded factual answers such as: 'What was the date of Waterloo?', 'How many lines in a sonnet?', and 'What is the chemical formula for silver?' Only the science lesson had a large proportion of questions forcing the pupils to reason. The number of really 'open' questions was tiny – that is, the teachers nearly always knew what they wanted to hear. Most teacher solicitations check that the pupils know something, or that they are able to reason it out, while the teacher knows the answer all along. Teachers hardly ever make genuine requests for information.

This is normal for the classroom and abnormal for everyday life. Teachers' questions are a good example of the point already made in Chapter 3, that classroom speech is unlike ordinary conversation. Just as it would be rude in polite society to bellow 'Say that in French!' when a party guest told you he had just backed the Derby winner, so there are perfectly ordinary teacher questions which would be unaskable in everyday life. Thus, it is rare to demand of people 'What is the pluperfect of *avoir*?', 'What gas is produced when you add dilute HCl to magnesium?', or 'How do you spell rhododendron?' *unless you really do not know the answers*. Cross-questioning, checking up and interrogation are rude in everyday life, but the staple of classroom life.

The acceptability of this cross-questioning lies in the relation between the teacher and the knowledge base. As long as knowledge is the exclusive possession of the teacher she has the duty to monitor the versions of that knowledge being acquired by the pupils. Once knowledge is located elsewhere, the nature of the teacher's questioning is free to change. This is not to say that it does.

Earlier in this volume we have seen that curriculum developers who intended to shift the focus and control of knowledge away from the teacher have run into difficulties. Few teachers are actually behaving as the curriculum developers intended. At classroom level, new patterns of questioning have to be organized which will reflect the new foci and control of knowledge. This was recognized long ago by the late Hilda Taba. When implementing a new social science curriculum for junior schools in California she not only provided materials but also trained the teachers to *ask different kinds of questions* (Verduin, 1972). Had the other curriculum developers recognized the importance of Taba's insights, many of the teething troubles of the British movement (see Whiteside, 1977) might have been avoided. It took ten years for the idea to re-emerge over here, with the work of the Ford Teaching Project. Walker and Adelman (1975b) include the insights of this work in an accessible form. They suggest a typology of teaching strategies, based on their years of research in all types of classroom, which allows us to see clearly the relationship between teacher, pupil, knowledge base and questioning strategy that lies at the heart of classroom negotiations.

Questions and content

Walker and Adelman locate their teaching strategies along two dimensions, which they call 'definition' and 'open v. closed content'. Definition, a word with deliberate photographic connotations, refers to the degree of specification of the pupil's role. When there is high definition, the pupil's role (a *positional* one) is to provide right answers – to play verbal 'ping pong' with the teacher. Where the role has low definition (i.e. is fuzzy), and is therefore *personal* not positional, the correct answers to questions are not clear, and the pupil role has more flexibility and ambiguity. The orthogonal dimension refers to the organization of lesson content in relation to the pupils. If it is 'open' the pupil is genuinely engaged in negotiating knowledge, if it is closed the content is organized into tight, logical steps over which the pupil has no control. (There are, of course, connections with the Bernsteinian notions of classification and frame outlined in Chapter 2.) Walker and Adelman locate three questioning strategies within their matrix as follows:

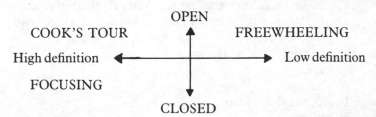

(Adapted from Walker and Adelman, 1975b, p. 47)

The authors have no name for the style which would occupy the fourth quadrant, nor is it easy to imagine what such a discourse

127

would look like. Brian Davies (1976, p. 170) has called it 'the promised land', and my students have nicknamed it 'the black hole'. The other three styles are easy to visualize.

Focusing is what most teachers are doing most of the time. The pupil's role is to give the right answer (high definition) and the right answer is logically determined by the teacher (content closed). The teacher is leading the class to converge on one right answer, which is predetermined. The following extract from Barnes (1971, p. 43) shows focusing perfectly:

T: Sand dunes. They're usually in an unusual . . . a specific shape . . . a special shape . . . Does anybody know what shape they are? Not in straight lines . . .

P: They're like hills.

T: Yes, they're like low hills.

P: They're all humpy up and down.

T: Yes, they're all humpy up and down.

P: They're like waves.

T: Good, they're like waves.

P: They're like . . .

T: They're a special shape.

P: They're like boulders . . . sort of go up and down getting higher and higher.

T: I don't know about getting higher and higher.

P: Sort of like pyramids.

T: Mmm . . . wouldn't call them pyramids, no.

P: They're in a semi-circle.

T: Ah, that's getting a bit nearer. They're often in a semi-circle and nearly always . . . we call them . . . well, it's part of a semi-circle . . . What do we call part of a semi-circle? . . . You think of the moon . . . perhaps you'll get the shape.

P: Water.

T: No, not shaped like water . . . Yes?

P: An arc.

T: An arc . . . oh, we're getting ever so much nearer.

P: Crescent.

T: A crescent shape. Have you heard that expression . . . a

crescent shape? I wonder if anybody could draw me a crescent shape on the board. Yes, they're nearly all that shape.

Cook's Tour describes a discourse which still has right answers, but in which the topic is shifted in an unpredictable manner. *Freewheeling* means that the teacher allows the class to contribute in unpredictable ways and, by definition, does not label pupil contributions as right and wrong. Examples of these questioning styles can be found in Walker and Adelman (1975b, pp. 47–51).

Of course, as we have already seen from the research evidence about classroom discourse, most teachers spend most of their time lecturing and then focusing. It can therefore be argued that in most schools focusing is the only discourse pattern pupils would recognize *as teaching*. Both the Cook's Tour and Free-wheeling are likely to be seen by pupils as disturbing departures from accepted, and acceptable, teacher practice. Cook's Tours are at least teacher-led, and therefore less disturbing than Freewheeling, which many pupils see as 'leading the teacher astray', or 'getting the teacher off the point', rather than a genuine educational exercise. This is not to say the pupils are correct – merely that most schools have led pupils to believe that listening to lectures and focusing are learning, while other activities are diversionary. Thus in many schools the teacher who tried to freewheel would be classified as 'easily led', and therefore 'soft'.

Of course pupils differ in the reaction to, and acceptance of, various teaching styles. Some are more willing to adapt themselves than others. Some will listen to a freewheeling discussion happily, but not want to take part, while others find focusing restrictive and try to broaden the control over knowledge. Yet others find any deviation from lecturing and focused questioning a 'waste of time' and react accordingly – switching off or disrupting attempts at change. Sarah Tann (1981) studied pupils who were asked to work cooperatively in small groups. She found that the ten-year-old children did not regard what they did as *work* or *learning* at all. Ninety-five children were involved, and ninety said they had enjoyed the tasks. But as Tann found:

> In experimental group work it was not facts, but opinions and interpretations which were exchanged, and this, by the pupils' criteria, was not 'learning' . . . The majority of the pupils, when asked what they thought they had learnt or gained from group work, replied that they gained nothing.

The students at Swidler's (1979) two free high schools held exactly the opposite view, feeling discussion *was* learning. Some pupils will favour one type of role in some subjects and another in other curriculum areas; or react differently to different teachers' attempts at innovatory classroom styles. These individual and sub-groups' differences in pupil perspective and strategy have hardly been researched at all, but understanding them is an important part of understanding classroom processes.

Individual differences

The number and type of contributions a pupil makes in lessons is directly related to the power of her resources and her perspectives on appropriate classroom behaviour.

The most famous work on student perspectives and strategies, carried out by Becker and his collaborators (1961 and 1968), concentrated on discovering beliefs and practices common to all students: to the whole student body. They deliberately did not establish the ways in which different sub-groups of students, or different individuals, construed the same situations in varying ways. Yet there must have been such variations. Classroom researchers have spent much time and effort on differentiating teachers: at first merely dichotomizing 'traditional' versus 'progressive' teachers, but now producing typologies of up to twelve styles (Bennett, 1976). Far less time and energy has been expended on pupil styles. Galton and Simon (1980) used the systematic observation schedule devised by Boydell called the Pupil Record, to separate four different pupil work patterns: attention seekers; intermittent workers; solitary workers; and quiet collaborators. Each of these types behaved differently in the classroom, but the ORACLE research did not collect their perspectives on schooling so we do not know if they felt differently. What is needed is a body of research where pupils are observed and interviewed, so that what they do, and how they account for it, can be analysed with allowances for their differences across various subjects and teachers.

The sociological attention on sub-cultural and individual differences in classroom behaviour has mostly focused on the disruptive activities of bored or hostile pupils. Willis (1977) for example describes with great gusto boys playing up in class, and Metz (1978) spends time on how low-stream pupils challenge teachers. This work is a legitimate topic of enquiry, but it is equally important to examine differential learning styles among basically successful, pro-school pupils, as in some tentative work of my own carried out at St Luke's. The type of analysis I am advocating can be demonstrated by the following discussion of a 'critical incident' I observed in a biology lesson. Two contrasting personal styles are vividly juxtaposed. In this particular lesson the class were coming to the end of a period of work on photosynthesis. Mrs Linnaeus wanted to complete the work by doing the experiment with sunlight and silver paper, which proves that light is necessary for photosynthesis to occur. (The experiment consists of covering leaves with silver foil with holes cut in it, exposing patches of leaf to the light. After a week or so the leaves are tested for starch, which is found in the exposed parts of the leaves and not in the covered parts.)

Mrs Linnaeus shouts for quiet and announces the last experiment.

Sharon: Good!

Mrs L: (Ignores Sharon, explains why they are doing it.) If we cover the leaves with silver foil and leave them for a few days what will happen to them?

Zoe: No sunlight can get through, so there won't be any starch.

Mrs L: (Accepts that – states it formally as a hypothesis. Asks what would happen if they cut holes in the foil.)

Karen: You'll get starch in the holes and not anywhere else.

Mrs L: (Accepts that – states it formally as an hypothesis. Asks for volunteers to cut and cover leaves.) You can cut your initials out if you like, then if it works you'll see your initials outlined in iodine.

Mary, Karen and Janice volunteer, and come to the front to get on with it. The others revert to their own activities . . . Michelle puts up her hand. Mrs Linnaeus acknowledges her . . .

Michelle: Mrs Linnaeus, *I* don't see how that will prove it – it could be all sorts of other things we don't know anything about.
Mrs L: (Comes down the lab to Michelle's bench. Asks her to expand her question, explain what she doesn't see.)
Michelle: Well, you said if there was starch in the bare patches it would mean there was . . . it was because of the light, but it could be the chemicals in the foil, or something we know nothing about.
Sharon: (butts in) Of course it'll prove it, we wouldn't be wasting our time doing the experiment if it didn't.
Mrs L: I don't think that's a very good reason, Sharon . . . (She laughs and then goes into great detail about experimental design, the atomic structure of carbohydrates, and other things in an attempt to satisfy Michelle. Few other girls listen, Henrietta does.)
Mrs L: You look worried Lorraine.
Lorraine: (Says she isn't.)

This incident crystallizes several issues important for classroom research, and raises several of the problems associated with pupil reactions to new styles of teaching. First, it shows the pitfalls inherent in guided discovery science in the schools. Mrs Linnaeus is caught between two challenges to the way she has 'stage-managed' her lesson. Her Scylla, Sharon, has seen through the guided discovery illusion and laid bare its true nature. She has seen that it is really heavily teacher structured and instrumental, and therefore their discovery is not 'real science'. Michelle, her Charybdis, accepts the illusion of real science, and challenges the adequacy of the experimental design from that angle. She wants to know whether their design meets the criteria of scientific proof. Both challenges are fundamental, because both attack the stage management which is essential for guided discovery in the schools where timetables, syllabuses and exams constantly intrude into the laboratory world. A much more detailed analysis of the problems of stage managed instruction can be found in Atkinson and Delamont (1976). Apart from the challenge to the stage management, which is not directly relevant here, it is clear that Sharon and Michelle have very different perspectives on, and therefore different strategies in, biology lessons. Sharon's perspective is instrumental and trusting: she accepts that Mrs Linnaeus knows what she is doing and that the pay-off will be worth the effort for her. In short, she expects Mrs Linnaeus to get her through the 'O' level syllabus. Michelle, on the other hand, is matching school science against real science (her parents were research scientists), and finding the former wanting. She has discovered a discrepancy in the teaching which, at the moment, concerns her more than quick progress through the syllabus. She wants a pay-off in intellectual satisfaction.

Michelle's queries are a serious challenge to Mrs Linnaeus's control over knowledge, because they highlight the essential tension between science in the real world and school learning. Mrs Linnaeus has to answer Michelle, because her doubts represent a fundamental challenge to her teaching. She believed in guided discovery and tried very hard to implement the method. However, she was operating with real time constraints and a syllabus to complete for a public examination. She has the choice of answering Michelle by exposing her stage management, or enlisting her greater knowledge of scientific theory to justify her procedures. By choosing the latter, which in part sustains the discovery illusion, she runs head-on into Sharon's exposure of her structure. Sharon's challenge is therefore dismissed with a laugh, although she does not actually say that Sharon is wrong! Had Mrs Linnaeus justified her choice of experimental design to Michelle in terms of constraints of time and equipment, Sharon's comment would have been supportive, as Sharon herself intended it to be. Of course, Mrs

Linnaeus had other options. She could have been angry, and asked Michelle if she had completed all her work, adding that she should 'get on and not ask stupid questions'. She could also have sent Michelle off to cover leaves with nineteen other light-excluding materials to test her own hypothesis, and this is probably the solution we should all like to see.

The very different perspectives held by Sharon and Michelle 'explain' why their classroom contributions are so different in form and content. (Further details of this incident and its background are provided in Delamont, 1976a.) Much more research effort needs to be spent in showing relationships between what actors think and what they do. This applies both to teachers and pupils – we need to understand why teachers have different classroom styles, and why pupils react differently to different staff – and these problems can only be tackled by detailed matching of perspectives and strategies. I found at St Luke's that the peer group who prided themselves on intellectual independence and creativity, and envisaged careers stretching on beyond university into research, were significantly more likely than their classmates to make tangential contributions aimed at broadening the focus of lessons. That is, they challenged the teacher's definition of, and control over, knowledge. Often, too, these girls had access to other sources of information – they had academic resources which could be used against the staff. Materials such as this on pupils' perspectives and resources 'explained' the frequency and types of classroom contributions made by the various girls.

Summary

This chapter has sketched some of the key strategies employed by teachers and pupils in the classroom, which reveal the kaleidoscopic complexity of the interaction. The 'crisis' faced by Mrs Linnaeus – two divergent pupil strategies – confronts many teachers in academic classes every day. In less intellectual spheres the teacher suffers from pupils who dispute her negotiated order, making instructional strategies difficult. Classroom researchers have a long way to go before such complex bargaining processes are understood – yet such understanding is essential for anyone who wishes to *change* teaching or learning. A failure to appreciate the subtleties of classroom interaction can vitiate the best-intentioned attempts at changing education. Classroom life has its own impetus and dynamics – which are ignored by the administrator or innovator at their peril. We all share certain cultural assumptions about teaching and learning which are hard to shed – hard for teachers, pupils and parents. We can negotiate together and bargain but our joint acts are not created in a vacuum – the class and political structure, and the belief system of our society, affect how we bargain and what we negotiate for.

6 The way forward

This postscript to the book offers some personal suggestions on the future of classroom research: not predictions of how I expect it to develop, but hopes as to how it might best be advanced. There are six ways in which the research could be improved, which are dealt with in the following order:

1. Coverage of the whole educational arena
2. The need for consolidation
3. Background reading
4. Interdisciplinary enquiry
5. Making the familiar strange
6. Generalizing and theorizing

While what follows is primarily the view of an educational ethnographer, the systematic observation research would also be enriched if the suggestions were followed.

1. Coverage of the whole educational arena

Classroom research has had a rather narrow, restricted empirical focus. Most work, both systematic and ethnographic, is done on children in state schools, of average ability, aged between 8–16, doing 'basic' subjects such as maths or English. There is very little work on private schools (such as religious institutions or elite boarding schools); on the very clever or the very dim; on the young or those over 16; and on areas of the curriculum such as PE, art, woodwork or photography. Very few researchers look at learning in classrooms outside schools: in adult education, in polytechnics, run by the Open University, in industry, in the health service. The potential trade-off from comparing different kinds of learning environments such as bedside teaching in the medical school and school science lessons (Atkinson and Delamont, 1976), or an industrial training unit for ESN adolescents with an adult education class (Atkinson and Shone, 1982) is considerable. It is also important that enough data on schooling are collected to provide a rounded picture of learning experiences. Junior school pupils spend a great deal of time on maths and language, but their other subjects are equally interesting. The training of remedial gymnasts is as important as the geography curriculum of fourteen-year-olds.

2. The need for consolidation

Two kinds of consolidation are included here: of methods and of findings. While replication in the strict experimental form normal in the physical sciences is rarely possible in classroom research, it is feasible to plan new studies so they relate in a principled way to previous investigations. The proliferation of dozens of different coding schedules for classroom interaction which have not been devised so the data they produce are comparable is one example of a lack of consolidation. In ethnographic studies there is a parallel tendency to assume that a topic has been 'done' when one researcher has looked at it. One study of occupational therapists in training does not exhaust the research area. Classroom research looks like a well-researched area, but in fact, because of a lack of consolidation, it is rather like a large lake which has developed a very thin coating of ice. It looks solid, but the research coverage is not thick enough to bear our weight.

3. Background reading

In part the lack of consolidation is due to the failure of researchers to read widely enough either in the literature on research methods or that on empirical findings. American researchers are unlikely to have read material from outside the USA, British scholars are poor in their grasp of overseas studies, and it appears that only Australian classroom observers have actually kept up with the field. (See, for example, Bullivant, 1978 and Smith, 1980.) The ethnographic researchers specializing in curriculum evaluation have neglected to read the literature on ethnographic research methods as both Delamont (1978) and Shipman (1982) have pointed out. Failing to read the literature leads inexorably to constant reinventions of the wheel and that wastes research time and money that could be put to better use.

There are now several papers which cover the existing literature on school and classroom ethnography, which new recruits and old hands could do well to read. Wilcox (1982) has covered all the literature in the American tradition of educational anthropology, and Borman (1981) has done a slighter, but still useful job for the American school ethnographies by sociologists. Doyle and Good (1982) and Karweit (1981) are insiders' perspectives on the 'time on task' literature, and Louis Smith (1983) has pulled together the different uses of ethnography in education with an American focus. Martyn Hammersley (1980, 1982) has produced two comprehensive accounts of the sociological literature on schools and classrooms in Britain, while Hargreaves (1980) contains reviews of the systematic observation research by Donald McIntyre (1980) and that on classroom language by Tony Edwards (1980). A comparison of the sociological and anthropological literatures is made in Atkinson and Delamont (1980), and my paper 'All to familiar?' (Delamont, 1981) is a controversial critique of the sociological research to date. Reading these essays would provide any interested person with a fair idea of the state of the art.

4. Interdisciplinary enquiry

This also means reading. Researchers must learn to read outside their immediate subject area to discover what members of other disciplines are doing. It is not possible to use the insights of other work if you have not read it! The findings of researchers from different backgrounds are often surprisingly complementary, but one has to read them before the parallels and confirmations are obvious. The work of Bennett (1976) and of Sharp and Green (1975) on elementary education is a good example of two pieces of work done from different perspectives in mutual isolation which can be read together with profit.

Interdisciplinary enquiry could be interpreted to mean research teams of different specialists, lead by a polymath qualified to be psychologist, linguist, anthropologist and so forth. Having worked in three self-styled interdisciplinary departments I do not recommend this approach to the classroom investigator. Under stress everyone retreats into their discipline and defends it like a barricade. Rather I hope researchers will pursue the type of enquiry they are at home with, but, at the same time, read other work and discuss classrooms with colleagues from other backgrounds. The sociologist in the classroom should remain a sociologist, but she should read what linguists, anthropologists, psychologists and ethologists are saying about classrooms.

5. Making the familiar strange

One fundamental task of social science is to subject 'common sense', 'taken-for-granted' reality to critical scrutiny. This means struggling to make familiar scenes, events and roles strange. Various strategies for doing this are described elsewhere (Delamont, 1981; Hammersley and Atkinson, 1983). The necessity for this approach to research was spelt out in 1971 by Howard Becker:

> We may have understated a little the difficulty of observing contemporary classrooms. It is not just the survey method of educational testing or any of those things that keeps people

from seeing what is going on. I think, instead that it is first and foremost a matter of it all being so familiar that it becomes impossible to single out events that occur in the classroom as things that have occurred, even when they happen right in front of you. I have not had the experience of observing in elementary and high school classrooms myself, but I have in college classrooms and it takes a tremendous effort of will and imagination to stop seeing only the things that are conventionally 'there' to be seen. I have talked to a couple of teams of research people who have sat around in classrooms trying to observe and it is like pulling teeth to get them to see or write anything beyond what 'everyone' knows. (p. 10)

This statement was picked up in Britain by Walker and Adelman (1972), but has not been widely disseminated in sociology of education. The problem Becker posed is a crucial one. Everyone in educational research has been to school, many of them have been teachers, hence the scene is 'so familiar'. When Becker says that getting researchers to see or write things which are insightful is like 'pulling teeth', he is expressing feelings familiar to many research supervisors and project directors. The very 'ordinariness', 'routineness' and 'everydayness' of school and classroom life do indeed confound many researchers, who complain that they are bored, they cannot find anything to write down, and that 'nothing happens'. All ethnographic work is hard, but schools and classrooms do have a particular kind of familiarity that was beautifully captured by Philip Jackson (1968).

Becker does, therefore, have a point. However it is not, or should not be, any kind of terminal diagnosis. Because the classroom is familiar does not mean that the researcher passively accepts the difficulty. Rather the task of the social scientist is *to make the familiar strange*. Becker's brief note does not address itself to solutions for the familiarity, but it is important to find some, rather than merely bleat about 'will and imagination'. If we accept his diagnosis, we are left to find our own solutions. Apart from those already outlined in this chapter, it is also true that school-based research is greatly improved by drawing on material from non-educational settings.

Despite Goffman's insights and pioneering work, research has not used material on hospitals, factories or shops to draw parallels and contrasts with educational settings. Howard Becker and Blanche Geer's educational work is cited, but that on other contexts for work socialization and job learning (Geer, 1972) is not. Classic sociological work in the interactionist tradition (e.g. by Anselm Strauss, Julius Roth and John Lofland); by French structuralists and post-structuralists (e.g. Foucault) and others is ignored, even when important parallels exist. An inspection of the bibliographies of research in classroom interaction and school life reveals that frequently *only* educational studies are cited. When other fields of research are mined, insights usually result: as in the comparison drawn between teachers' typifications of pupils and staff categorization in an accident and emergency hospital ward drawn by Woods (1979, p. 175).

6. Generalizing and theorizing

Theoretical insight is noticeably lacking from most classroom research. Until we have a coherent theory, or theories, for the study of face-to-face interaction, it will always look messy and unsatisfying. Theoretical insights may grow out of the research ('grounded theory') or be distilled from more wide-ranging 'grand theory' such as the typologies of Basil Bernstein (Hannan, 1975; Hamilton, 1975). Both ways of generating theoretical insights into classroom life are appealing. My own views are expressed in the following passage written collaboratively with Paul Atkinson during a research project on industrial training units (see Atkinson and Delamont, 1985).

The overall approach of ethnographic work must rest on a comparative principle. If studies are not explicitly developed into more general frameworks, then they will be doomed to remain isolated 'one-off affairs', with no sense of cumulative knowledge or developing theoretical insight. If one is to adopt an essentially ethnographic approach to research, then the work will remain inadequate unless comparative perspectives are employed. This point concerning comparative perspectives relates directly to the issue of the generalizability of such research and its 'findings'. The analytic approach to such studies should be conceived of in terms of *formal* concepts – or, as Lofland (1971) calls them, *generic* problems.

These formal concepts are abstract, ideal-typical, notions which characterize features, problems and issues which may be common to a range of different concrete settings. A well known example of this sort of concept is Goffman's (1968a) formulation of the 'total institution' which he uses to portray features which are common to a wide variety of apparently diverse organizations (mental hospitals, monasteries, military camps, etc.). Thus Goffman's primary analysis of the mental hospital is developed through explicit and implicit comparison with these other institutions, which are shown, in *formal* terms, to have common features.

The development of such formal concepts thus frees the researcher from the potential straight-jacket of restricting attention only to the particular setting directly available to study. Indeed, the emphasis is, if anything, reversed. Ethnographers in sociology have sometimes been taxed with the charge of devoting too much attention to 'trivial', 'exotic' or 'bizarre' settings of everyday life, but these settings are used to illustrate and display the formal properties of social life. As Rock (1979) puts it:

> The career of the high school teacher, the organization of a ward for tuberculosis patients, the moral history of the taxi-dancer, the career of a mental patient, and transactions between police and juvenile delinquents present materials for the dissection of elementary social forms. They are explored to illuminate a simple grammar of sociation, a grammar whose rules give order to the allocation of territorial rights, the programming of timetables, and the meeting of diverse groups. More important, it is a grammar which is intended to provide recipes for an understanding of the abstract properties of social life. (p. 50)

Theory in this context is not a self-contained, de-contextualized activity. While the formal concepts are derived from concrete instances and settings, they are only recognizable, and are only realized in their concrete manifestations. There is a constant interplay between 'theory', 'method' and 'findings'. At the same time, if researchers are unwilling to grapple with the formal concepts and theories, then their work is doomed to be little more than a series of one-off, self-contained reports, all of which return to 'square one', conceptually speaking. Suffice it to say that all accounts of classrooms will be deficient until the theoretical aspects are properly developed.

Further reading

There are two areas of literature that may interest the reader: ethnographic methods and studies of schools and classrooms. Accordingly I have given a few examples of books in each category.

Ethnographic methods

Hammersley, Martyn and Atkinson, Paul A. (1983) *Ethnography: Principles in Practice*
This book has an extensive bibliography and is therefore a good route into this literature, much of which is neglected by educational researchers.

Burgess, Robert G. (ed.) (1982) *Field Research: A Sourcebook and Field Manual*
This is a recent, and extremely useful, collection of articles which give access to the overall research area.

Spradley, James P. (1980) *Participant observation*
This is a recent manual on how to do ethnography, which makes it seem possible, interesting and even discusses how to write up one's findings.

These three books will lead the reader into the research tradition of ethnography.

Studies of educational institutions

The bibliography includes references to many of the empirical studies of educational institutions. I have listed here, for special attention, a few monographs (books on one subject) and some collections of papers. The monographs are those I feel deserve to be read in their entirety, by anyone interested in life in educational institutions. The collections are those which will give a reader access to the various approaches to studying classrooms, such as the socio-linguistic, the anthropological and so on.

The monographs I would recommend are:
Atkinson, Paul (1981) *The Clinical Experience*
Bullivant, B. M. (1978) *The Way of Tradition: Life in an Orthodox Jewish School*
Hargreaves, David H. *et al.* (1975) *Deviance in Classrooms*
King, Ronald (1978) *All Things Bright and Beautiful*
Metz, Mary (1978) *Classrooms and Corridors*
Swidler, Ann (1979) *Organization without Authority: Dilemmas of Social Control in Free Schools*
Wolcott, Harry F. (1973) *The Man in the Principal's Office*

Delamont, Sara (ed.) (1984) *Readings on Interaction in the Classroom*
This is a collection of papers to accompany the present volume.

A parallel reader focusing on language in the school is also essential reading for classroom researchers:
Stubbs, Michael and Hillier, Hilary (eds) (1983) *Readings on Language, Schools and Classrooms*

There are several collections of papers which provide access to aspects of the literature: the anthropological approach to the study of schools and classrooms can be found in:
Spindler, George (ed.) (1982) *Doing the Ethnography of Schooling: Educational Anthropology in Action*

Work on bilingual classrooms can be found in:
Trueba, Henry T. *et al.* (eds) (1981) *Culture and the Bilingual Classroom*

The work on conversational analysis and similar perspectives is brought together in:
Green, Judith and Wallat, Cynthia (eds) (1981) *Ethnography and Language in Educational Settings*

There is a special issue of the journal *Educational Analysis* (vol. 2, no. 2, Winter 1980) which is devoted to different approaches to the study of classrooms. This makes a good starting point for the novice. A good route into the best of recent British sociological work can be found in two collections edited by Peter Woods (1980a and 1980b) called *Teacher Strategies* and *Pupil Strategies*. These volumes have papers by Ham-

145

mersley, Denscombe, Pollard, Andrew Hargreaves and Stephen Ball among others, and will give a good appreciation of the approach. Another similar collection is:

Hammersley, Martyn (ed.) (1983) *Ethnography of Schooling*

Autobiographical accounts

An interesting collection of autobiographical accounts of how ethnographic research was done by ten different scholars is:

Burgess, Robert G.(ed.) (1984) *The Research Process in Educational Settings*. Brighton: Falmer Books.

References and
name index

The numbers in italics after each entry refer to page numbers within this book.

Adams, R. S. and Biddle, B. J. (1970) *Realities of Teaching.* New York: Holt, Rinehart and Winston. *38*

Adelman, Clem (1975) Developing pictures for other frames. In G. Chanan and S. Delamont (eds) *Frontiers of Classroom Research. 71*

Adorno. T. W. *et al.* (1950) *The Authoritarian Personality.* New York: Harper and Row. *18*

Amidon, E. J. and Hough, J. B. (eds) (1967) *Interaction Analysis.* Reading, Mass.: Addison-Wesley. *16*

Ashton, P. (1981) Primary teachers' aims, 1969–77. In B. Simon and J. Willcocks (eds) *Research and Practice in the Primary Classroom. 69*

Ashton, P. *et al.* (1975) *The Aims of Primary Education: A Study of Teachers' Opinions.* London: Macmillan. *68–9*

Atkinson, Paul (1981) *The Clinical Experience.* Aldershot: Gower. *145*

Atkinson, Paul (1983) The reproduction of professional community. In R. Dingwall and P. Lewis (eds) *The Sociology of the Professions: Lawyers, Doctors and Others.* London: Macmillan. *15*

Atkinson, Paul and Delamont, Sara (1976) Mock-ups and cock-ups. In Martyn Hammersley and Peter Woods (eds) *The Process of Schooling.* London: Routledge and Kegan Paul. *25, 133, 137*

Atkinson, Paul and Delamont, S. (1980) The two traditions in educational ethnography: sociology and anthropology compared. *British Journal of Sociology of Education 1*: 2, 139–52. *138*

Atkinson, Paul and Delamont, S. (1985) Bread and dreams or bread and circuses? In M. Shipman (ed.) *Educational Research: Principles, Policies, and Practice.* Brighton: Falmer Books. *141*

Atkinson, Paul and Shone, David (1982) Industrial training for slow learners: an ethnographic study. *Education for Development* 6: 3, 25–30. Reprinted in L. Barton and S. Tomlinson (eds) *Special Education*. London: Harper and Row. *137, 141–2*

Ball, Stephen (1980) Initial encounters in the classroom. In Peter Woods (ed.) (1980b) *Pupil Strategies*. *111–12*
Ball, Stephen (1981) *Beachside Comprehensive*. Cambridge: Cambridge University Press. *84*
Ball, Stephen and Lacey, Colin (1980) Subject disciplines as the opportunity for group action: a measured critique of subject sub-cultures. In P. Woods (ed.) (1980a) *Teacher Strategies*. *61*
Banks, Olive (1968) *The Sociology of Education*. London: Batsford (2nd edn, 1971; 3rd edn, 1976). *22*
Barnes, D. (1971) *Language, the Learner and the School* (2nd edn). Harmondsworth: Penguin. *125, 128*
Becker, H. S. (1952) Social class variations in the teacher-pupil relationship. *Journal of Educational Sociology* 25: 4, 451–65. *71, 74*
Becker, H. S. (1953) The teacher in the authority system of the public school. *Journal of Educational Sociology* 27: 128–41. *41, 60, 62–3*
Becker, H. S. (1971) Footnote. In M. Wax *et al.* (eds) *Anthropological Perspectives on Education*. New York: Basic Books. *139–40*
Becker, H. S. *et al.* (1961) *Boys in White*. Chicago: University of Chicago Press. *29, 44, 100–7, 130*
Becker, H. S. *et al.* (1968) *Making the Grade*. New York: Wiley. *29, 44, 100–7, 130*
Bellack, A. A. *et al.* (1966) *The Language of the Classroom*. New York: Teachers College Press. *53–4, 119, 124, 125*
Bennett, S. Neville (1976) *Teaching Styles and Pupil Progress*. London: Open Books. *21, 130, 139*
Bennett, S. Neville (1980) *Open-plan Schools*. London: NFER/Nelson. *21, 35*
Bennett, S. Neville and Desforges, Charles (1984) *The Quality of Pupil Learning Experiences*. London: Erlbaum. *67*
Bennett, S. Neville and Jordan, J. (1975) A typology of teaching styles in primary schools. *British Journal of Educational Psychology* 45: 1, 20–8. *72*
Bennett, S. Neville and McNamara, David (eds) (1979) *Focus on Teaching*. London: Longmans. *21*
Berlak, Ann and Harold (1981) *Dilemmas of Schooling*. London: Methuen. *70, 71, 74*
Bernstein, Basil (1971) On the classification and framing of educational knowledge. In M. F. D. Young (ed.) *Knowledge and Control*. *42–3*
Beynon, John and Atkinson, Paul (1984) Pupils as data-gatherers: mucking and sussing. In S. Delamont (ed.) (1984) *Readings on Interaction in the Classroom*. London: Methuen. *100*

Beynon, J. and Delamont, S. (1984) The sound and the fury. In N. Frude and H. Gault (eds) *Disruptive Behaviour in Schools.* Chichester: Wiley. *112*

Blumer, H. (1966) Sociological implications of the thought of George Herbert Mead. *American Journal of Sociology, 71*: 535–44. *26, 28*

Borman, Kathryn (1981) Review of recent case studies on equity and schooling. In R. G. Corwin (ed.) *Research on Educational Organizations* (volume 2 in the series *Research in Sociology of Education and Socialization*). Greenwich, Conn.: JAI Press. *138*

Boydell, Deanne (1974) Teacher-pupil contact in junior classrooms. *British Journal of Educational Psychology, 44*: 313–18. *117–19, 121–3, 130*

Braithwaite, E. R. (1959) *To Sir, with Love.* London: Bodley Head. *94*

Bream, F. (1970) *Chalk Dust and Chewing Gum.* London: Collins. *109–11, 123*

Brophy, J. E. and Good, T. L. (1974) *Teacher-Student Relationships.* New York: Holt, Rinehart and Winston. *64, 65, 86*

Brown, Roger (1965) *Social Psychology.* London: Collier-Macmillan. *48, 92*

Bullivant, B. M. (1978) *The Way of Tradition: Life in an Orthodox Jewish School.* Victoria, Australia: Australian Council for Educational Research. *40, 42, 52–3, 73, 84, 98–9, 107, 138, 145*

Burgess, R. G. (ed.) (1982) *Field Research: A Sourcebook and Field Manual.* London: Allen and Unwin. *144*

Cane, B. and Schroeder, C. (1970) *The Teacher and Research.* Slough: NFER. *69*

Chanan, G. and Delamont, S. (eds) (1975) *Frontiers of Classroom Research.* Slough: NFER. *16, 21*

Cicourel, A. V. and Kitsuse, J. I. (1968) The social organization of the high school and deviant adolescent careers. In B. R. Cosin *et al.* (eds) (1971) *School and Society.* London: Routledge and Kegan Paul. *31*

Clarricoates, Katherine (1980) The importance of being Ernest . . . Tom . . . Jane: the perception and categorization of gender conformity and gender deviation in primary schools. In R. Deem (ed.) *Schooling for Women's Work.* London: Routledge and Kegan Paul. *66*

Coleman, James S. (1961) *The Adolescent Society.* Glencoe: The Free Press. *83*

Davies, Brian (1973) On the contribution of organizational analysis to the study of educational institutions. In R. Brown (ed.) *Knowledge, Education and Cultural Change.* London: Tavistock. *39*

Davies, Brian (1976) *Social Control and Education.* London: Methuen. *22, 128*

Davies, Brian (1981) Schools as organizations and the organization of

London: University of London Press. 55

Strauss, Anselm et al. (1964) Psychiatric Ideologies and Institutions. London: Collier-Macmillan. 28, 30, 34, 39, 59

Strauss, Anselm (1978) Negotiations: Varieties, Contexts, Processes, and Social Order. San Francisco: Jossey-Bass. 28

Stuart, S. (1969) Say. London: Nelson. 115

Stubbs, Michael (1975) Teaching and talking. In G. Chanan and S. Delamont (eds) Frontiers of Classroom Research. 56

Stubbs, Michael (1983) Language, Schools and Classrooms (2nd edn). London: Methuen.

Stubbs, Michael and Delamont, Sara (eds) (1976) Explorations in Classroom Observation. Chichester: Wiley. 21

Stubbs, Michael and Hillier, Hilary (eds) (1983) Readings on Language, Schools and Classrooms. London: Methuen. 56, 125, 145

Sussman, Leila (1977) Tales out of School. Philadelphia: Temple University Press. 33, 42

Swidler, Ann (1979) Organization without Authority: Dilemmas of Social Control in Free Schools. Cambridge, Mass.: Harvard University Press. 42, 55, 67, 99–100, 130, 145

Tann, Sarah (1981) Grouping and group work. In B. Simon and J. Willcocks (eds) Research and Practice in the Primary Classroom. 129–30

Torode, B. (1976) Teacher's talk and classroom discipline. In M. Stubbs and S. Delamont (eds) Explorations in Classroom Observation. 90, 124

Trueba, Henry T., Guthrie, Grace Pung and Au, Kathryn Hu-Pei (eds) (1981) Culture and the Bilingual Classroom: Studies in Classroom Ethnography. Rowley, Mass.: Newbury House. 145

Verduin, J. R. (1972) Teaching strategies for cognitive growth. In E. Stones and S. Morris (eds) Teaching Practice. London: Methuen. 126

Walker, Rob (1972) The sociology of education and life in school classrooms. International Review of Education, 18: 32–43. 21–3

Walker, Rob and Adelman, Clem (1972) Towards A Sociography of Classrooms. Final report to the SSRC on Grants Nos HR 996/1 and HR 1442/1. 140

Walker, Rob and Adelman, Clem (1975a) Interaction analysis in informal classrooms: a critical comment on the Flanders system. British Journal of Educational Psychology, 45: 1, 73–6. 20

Walker, Rob and Adelman, Clem (1975b) A Guide to Classroom Observation. London: Methuen. 93, 119, 126–9

Walker, Rob and Adelman, Clem (1976) Strawberries. In M. Stubbs and S. Delamont (eds) Explorations in Classroom Observation. 31–2

Wax, Murray and Wax, Rosalie (1971) Great tradition, little tradition, and formal education. In M. Wax and S. Diamond and F. Gearing (eds) *Anthropological Perspectives on Education*, New York: Basic Books.

Werthman, C. (1963) Delinquents in schools. In B. R. Cosin *et al.* (eds) (1971) *School and Society*. London: Routledge and Kegan Paul. *81, 82, 90–1, 105*

Whiteside, M. Thomas (1977) *The Sociology of Educational Innovation*. London: Methuen. *126*

Whiteside, M. T. and Mathieson, M. (1971) The secondary modern school in fiction. *British Journal of Educational Studies, XIX*: 3, 283–92. *109*

Wilcox, Kathleen (1982a) Differential socialization in the classroom: implications for equal opportunity. In G. Spindler (ed.) *Doing the Ethnography of Schooling. 68, 138*

Wilcox, Kathleen (1982b) Ethnography as a methodology and its applications to the study of schooling: a review. In G. Spindler (ed.) *Doing the Ethnography of Schooling. 68, 138*

Willes, Mary (1981) Learning to take part in classroom interaction. In P. French and M. Maclure (eds) *Adult-Child Conversation*. London: Croom Helm. *113*

Willis, Paul (1977) *Learning to Labour*. Farnborough: Saxon House. *78, 80, 82, 85, 105, 131*

Wober, M. (1971) *English Girls' Boarding Schools*. London: Allen Lane. *41*

Wolcott, Harry F. (1973) *The Man in the Principal's Office*. New York: Holt, Rinehart and Winston. *145*

Woods, Peter (1979) *The Divided School*. London: Routledge and Kegan Paul. *57–8, 70, 84, 85, 87, 92, 97, 141*

Woods, Peter (ed.) (1980a) *Teacher Strategies*. London: Croom Helm. *71,115, 145*

Woods, Peter (ed.) (1980b) *Pupil Strategies*. London: Croom Helm. *71, 115, 145*

Wragg, E. C. (1973) A study of student teachers in the classroom. In G. Chanan (ed.) *Towards a Science of Teaching*. Slough: NFER. *117, 120, 122, 124*

Young, M. F. D. (ed.) (1971) *Knowledge and Control*. London: Collier-Macmillan.

Young, M. F. D. (1976) School science: innovation or alienation? In P. Woods and M. Hammersley (eds) *School Experience*. London: Croom Helm. *52–3*

Subject index